I0135174

TREASURE IN HEAVEN

A Study of the Sermon on the Mount
Using the Four Senses of Scripture

✠

Barry R. Pearlman

TREASURE IN HEAVEN

A Study of the
Sermon on the Mount
Using the
Four Senses of Scripture

⊕

SECOND
SPRING

First published
by Second Spring, 2014
www.secondspring.co.uk
an imprint of Angelico Press
© Barry R. Pearlman 2014

All rights reserved

No part of this book may be reproduced or transmitted,
in any form or by any means, without permission.

For information, address:
Angelico Press
4709 Briar Knoll Dr.
Kettering, OH 45429
angelicopress.com

978-1-62138-089-4 (pbk)
978-1-62138-090-0 (ebook)

Cover image: Jacques Callot (1592–1635)
The Sermon on the Mount, 1635
etching on paper

Cover design: Michael Schrauzer

For Stratford

CONTENTS

A Prefatory Note

W E START WITH a supreme principle of Catholic faith that Jesus Christ is the founder and head of the Church. Since the Incarnation was not an accident, then neither was the Church an accident. It is unthinkable that he who is all powerful and who does all things well would have abandoned his Church to be blown about by every wind of change, to be deceived, or to fall into error. Rather, Jesus would protect and guide the Church he suffered and died for. This follows as a necessary and simple deduction from who Christ is; and would stand alone as true, were it not also for the fact that Our Lord himself said so: "the Holy Spirit, whom the Father will send in my name, will teach you everything. . . ." (Jn. 14:26). And again: "Anyone who hears you [the apostles] hears me. . . ." (Lk. 10:16). Thus we shall respect the canon of scripture as the inspired and authoritative word of God to be read and understood within the tradition and mind of the Church.[1]

From this follows our second principle: should any scholar or theologian dispute the Church's doctrinal or moral understanding of sacred scripture, the onus would fall on that person to prove one's position. But such a proof cannot be carried out in practice because of a number of theorems from philosophy of science that

---

1. "God graciously arranged that the things he had once revealed for the salvation of all peoples should remain in their entirety, throughout the ages, and be transmitted to all generations. Therefore, Christ the Lord, in whom the entire Revelation of the most high God is summed up . . . commanded the apostles to preach the Gospel . . . to communicate the gifts of God to all men. This Gospel was to be the source of all saving truth and moral discipline. This was faithfully done. Thus, the apostolic preaching, which is expressed in a special way in the inspired books, was to be preserved in a continuous line of succession until the end of time. . . . The spouse of the incarnate Word, which is the Church, is taught by the Holy Spirit. . . . The sacred Synod encourages those sons of the Church who are engaged in biblical studies constantly to renew their efforts...with complete dedication and in accordance with the mind of the Church." *Dei Verbum*, 7, 8, 23 *passim*.

have put severe restrictions upon what can be claimed to be known from empirical methods alone. These will be examined in the first chapter where it will be shown that it is *impossible to demonstrate* that any one of these critical methods, by itself, will ever arrive at a conclusive solution to such problems as, for example: what are the written or oral sources behind the Gospels, in what order were they written, or how they were edited, etc. Higher criticism continues to remain conjecture without independent objective proof.

Thirdly, on this basis we can reject any notion that God's revelation was given *only* for the scholarly elite. We feel the scriptures are for everyone to read *providing they are read with the mind of the Church,* as we said in our first principle and as Our Lord confirms: "I bless you, Father . . . for hiding these things from the learned and the clever and revealing them to little children" (Mt 11:25). Yet, sacred scripture has the power and depth to involve the most penetrating intellects, for great theologies, literature, art, and religious orders have flourished from its pages.

Since one always finds hidden depths within scripture, we shall adopt the tradition of attending to its Four Senses.[2] These senses involve the whole person in understanding its teaching. First there is the literal sense that corresponds to our physical reality. It is based on the meaning of the words themselves according to their normal usage, form, and context. All other senses of scripture are founded upon the literal sense. The moral (tropological) sense instructs us to live just and holy lives. Speaking to our relationship with others and with God, it enkindles the moral virtues of our souls. The allegorical (or typological) sense helps us to understand the significance of events as they prefigure the Christ. This sense illuminates our minds and secures us in holy doctrine. Finally, the anagogical or mystical sense sparks our intuition and leads our hearts to God. Thus, the moral sense purges us of impurity; the allegorical illuminates our understanding; and the mystical invites us to unite with the Divine.

---

2. See the *Catechism of the Catholic Church,* 115–119.

A Prefatory Note

I would like to express my indebtedness to the late Stratford Calde-
cott, of blessed memory, whose idea was the basis for this project.
His invaluable encouragement, discussions, and suggestions have
been of inestimable help. He will be sadly missed.

The text of the sermon comes primarily from the *New Jerusalem
Bible* published and copyright © 1985 by Darton, Longman & Todd
Ltd and Doubleday, a division of Random House Inc. Any depar-
ture from this text or from its order is the author's own translation.

PART ONE
Interpretive Principles

1

Theology beyond Method

OUR ULTIMATE authority for everything in the Catholic faith is Our Lord Jesus Christ and that tradition received from him and handed on to the Church by his Apostles. This deposit even embraces the interpretive or hermeneutical precedents set by them. So it is to them we must first look for those principles to guide us in our feeble human attempts to plumb the depths of sacred scripture. We shall, therefore, start with Jesus and Paul before moving on to examine the growth and content of medieval exegesis. After this we shall witness the rise and demise of historical criticism and of method in general. The rise of *ressourcement* and its recovery of the four senses of scripture will complete this chapter.

The Traditional Interpretation of Scripture

The Teaching of Jesus

What first strikes us about the manner of Jesus' teaching to his disciples is that "he would not speak to them except in parables" (Mk. 4:34; Mt. 13:34, 22:1; Jn. 16:25). Even so, this parabolic and figurative form of teaching was but a development of that classical Jewish commentary known as *midrash* (from *darash* to seek). There were two sorts of midrash. *Halakhah* (from *halakh* to walk) embodied those rules of conduct that the children of Israel should follow during their walk with God; while *haggadah* (from *higgidh* to tell) included narrative, legends, doctrines, admonitions, consolations, and expressions of hope for future redemption. Its forms were as varied and lively as its content: parables and allegories; metaphors, maxims, and prayers; satirical tales and polemical dialogues; as well as hyperboles, and puns. Yet their purpose was always to interpret the ways of God.

Jesus' use of parables also embodied this rich haggadic panoply, which most fittingly served his proclamation of the kingship, reign or sovereignty of God. Although, while the forms of Jesus' teaching were mainly haggadic, nonetheless he also declared that it was never his intention to abandon halakhah: "Do not imagine that I have come to abolish the Law or the Prophets. I have come not to abolish but to complete them. I tell you . . . not one dot, not one little stroke, is to disappear from the Law until its purpose is achieved" (Mt. 5:17–18).

In his colorful and dynamic manner of teaching, Jesus appealed to the entire person and to one's life in all its aspects. Within this spectrum one cannot help but detect those nascent four senses that became so characteristic of the Middle Ages. To begin with, it is noteworthy that at times Jesus did adopt a literal or historical interpretation of the Hebrew scriptures. Our Lord's references to Adam, Noah and the flood, Abraham and his descendents, Moses' receipt of the Ten Commandments and his transmission of the law, the exploits of David and Solomon, and the persecutions of the prophets were plainly historical in intent. Secondly, the moral or halakhic sense was often apparent in Our Lord's clear precepts, as we shall encounter in his Sermon on the Mount. But for the moment it will suffice to be reminded of his repetition of the Ten Commandments to the rich young ruler (Mk. 10:17–22) or his moral criteria at the Last Judgement (Mt. 25:31ff). The third figurative or allegorical sense has many examples: from the figure of Jonah in the belly of the whale foreshadowing Our Lord's three days in the tomb, the elevation of the bronze serpent near Oboth as a figure of the crucifixion, and the portrayal of Elijah as a precursor of St. John the Baptist; to the parables of the soils, the prodigal son, the wicked tenants, and the enacted cursing of the fig tree. Whether the figurative meanings are taken from history, personal haggadah, or observation, the use of the allegorical sense is the most obvious feature of Our Lord's rabbinic style. Finally, the mystical sense especially pervades those tender expressions of Jesus' intimate relationship with the Father as poignantly revealed in his profound sacerdotal prayer

(Jn. 17). But perhaps the deepest expression of mystery is his representation of the Passover symbolism during the Last Supper. These four senses—the literal, moral, allegorical, and mystical—were immediately perceived by the astute and sensitive minds of the early Church Fathers. But it is Paul whom they considered the founder and exemplar of Christian allegory.

Paul's Use of Scripture

One would expect that St. Paul, the student of the distinguished Gemaliel, would be familiar with the rabbinic styles of teaching. But in his hands allegory became distinctively Christian. For St. Paul the spiritual sense of scripture (allegorical and mystical) were principally applied to communicate and illuminate Christ. All scriptural typology was a prolegomenon to the Son of God, which was fulfilled in the life and person of Jesus.

A typical example is Paul's allegorical interpretation of Sarah and Hagar: "These things are allegorized (*hattina estin allegoroumena*)." Abraham had two sons: one by the slave girl Hagar and one by Sarah the freewoman. These women signify two covenants. The old covenant given on Mount Sinai (i.e., Hagar whose children were born into slavery) represents Jerusalem under the old covenant while Sarah, whose son was born under the promise, represents the new covenant under Christ (Ga. 4:21ff). Thus Paul develops by way of allegory his theme that Jewry continues to be under the slavery of the law of sin and death, while Christians are under the freedom of grace through Christ Jesus.

Another familiar example of Pauline allegory is his use of Adam, the first man and father of all the living, to "prefigure the One who is to come" (Ro. 5:14). As sin and death came through Adam, so forgiveness and resurrection unto eternal life come through Christ (1 Cor. 15:20ff). In a similar manner, a verse from Deuteronomy 21:22–23, which describes the accursed state of a man punished by being hung on a tree, was allegorized to prefigure Jesus' being condemned to hang upon the cross: He was made a curse for our sake so that in him the blessing of Abraham might come upon the Gentiles "so that we might receive the promised Spirit through faith" (Ga. 3:13–14). And again, the rock which Moses struck to obtain water to preserve his people in the desert is another foreshadowing of Christ, who was stricken also and from whose wounded side flowed the water of life (1 Cor. 10:4).

St. Paul's mystical employment of haggadah is made apparent in his profound analogy between the mystery of the Church, as the bride of Christ, and the sacrament of marriage (Ep. 5:21–33). In this passage he goes back to the creation account in Genesis which asserts that in marriage a man and a woman become one flesh "For this reason a man shall leave his father and mother and be joined to his wife, and the two shall become one flesh." (2:24). Paul concludes from this that men must love their wives as their own bodies as Christ loves the Church, communicating his grace to her, which is his body for he is her head. And similarly women should be receptive to their husbands as the Church is open to the grace of Christ: because we are members of his body. This reveals the sacramental character of the Church in which Christ the head is conjoined to the Church forming her members into one spiritual body through grace. Thus Paul makes the sacramental and generative nature of the marriage between a man and a woman the prefigurative and exemplary image of the substantial union of Christ and his Church in the Holy Spirit: "that she might be holy and without blemish." Paul declares this a great mystery.

St Paul, of course, also uses literal-historical allusions (such as those concerning Christ's bodily resurrection) and moral counsels (such as his advice to Timothy). But it is his allegorical and anagogical (or mystical) interpretations that influenced the Patristic and Medieval periods which followed.

Medieval Use of the Four Senses

The proliferation, application, and features of the four senses in medieval exegesis were so widespread and various, so penetrating and inventive, that we can hardly do justice to the topic here. Fr. Henri de Lubac (S.J.) in his epochal and definitive four-volume work has set the standard for some time to come. Here we shall give just a few of his numerous examples of the leading lights in the development of this imaginative and intriguing approach to scripture. We say "approach" because it could never be said to resemble those systematic, step-by-step, despiritualized methods so typical of modern exegesis. For it is of the nature of the four senses that they were intended to lead (exegesis comes from *ex hegeisthai*—to lead) the Biblical seeker beyond the literal and historical sense to an encounter with the living Word who is the fount of all wisdom. Our Lord has said: "You search the Scriptures . . . and it is they that bear witness to me" (Jn. 5:39). Or as St. Augustine affirmed: "Whatever doubt a human being has in mind on hearing God's Scriptures, let him not fall back from Christ; when Christ has been revealed in those words, let him understand that he has understood; but before he come to an understanding of Christ, let him not presume that he has understood."[1] The whole content of divine scripture is one book, and that one book is Christ, because all scripture speaks of him, and is fulfilled in him.

One may safely say that St. Irenaeus' principle, that scripture must be interpreted within the tradition of the Church,[2] imparted the context and justification for the utilization of Pauline allegory among the early Church Fathers. For on the one hand we have Irenaeus' foundation of the doctrine of the rule of faith, and on the other the Christian allegorical tradition handed on by St. Paul. Therefore, biblical commentators were free to seek for hidden meanings within scripture provided they exercised the rule of faith.

Origen (c. 185–254) must be credited as the principal advocate of the practice of seeking for the various senses of scripture. He thought that scripture, like man, has a body, soul, and spirit. The corporeal sense corresponded to history, the psychical to morality,

---

1. Quoted in de Lubac, *Medieval Exegesis,* vol. II, p. 93.
2. "It does not follow because men are endowed with greater and less degrees of intelligence, that they should therefore change the subject-matter [of the faith] itself, and should conceive of some other God besides Him who is the Framer, Maker, and Preserver of this universe, (as if He were not sufficient for them), or of another Christ, or another Only-begotten. But the fact referred to simply implies this, that one may [more accurately than another] bring out the meaning of those things which have been spoken in parables, and accommodate them to the general scheme of the faith; and explain [with special clearness] the operation and dispensation of God connected with human salvation…" (*Adversus Haereses.* 1:10, 1–2, c. AD 175–185).

and the spiritual to allegory or anagogy. These latter two were still conflated in their application, however. Origen was impatient with historical details: it was of no use to him to know, for example, that Abraham sat under the tree of Mambre, unless he could find some hidden meaning. So through a laboured etymology he arrived at the idea that "Mambre" means "keen sight," by which Abraham was enabled to see God. He understood the crossing of the Jordan in the book of Joshua to be a type of baptism, giving the anagogical sense that the parting of the Jordan will lead to the Promised Land through the services of priests. Even the five enemies of Joshua represented the five senses which must be vanquished lest they lead us into sin.

Origen was condemned as a heretic by Pope Vigilius in the sixth century for professing that Heavenly bodies were living powers, that human souls (including that of Christ) pre-existed, and the idea that salvation will finally be extended even to "the demons or to impious men." Clearly he did not remain within the rule of faith. Nevertheless his influence was immense—e.g., Jerome defended him, Rufinus translated him, and monasteries like San Giorgio, Clairvaux, and Signy preserved his works—since it was Origen who firmly established the search for hidden meanings in scripture as well as separating the various senses. Yet his determination to avoid the literal meaning often rendered his allegorizing somewhat arbitrary.

However, it was St. Bede (673–739) who provided us with the best example of traditional exegesis and who was the essential link between the so-called Dark Ages and the High Middle Ages. Born on the lands of the monastery at Wearmouth, he became a monk there and later of its sister monastery at Jarrow. To the duties of teaching and prayer, he added the study of science, literature, Latin, and Greek. His greatest work was his *Ecclesiastical History of the English People*, which covered the period from Julius Caesar's invasion to a period of relative peace in 731. It was to the study of the Bible that most of his energies were devoted. He died while completing a translation into English of the Gospel of John.

It is in Bede's commentary on the book of Samuel that we detect the establishment of the four senses:

[The disciples of the Lord] gave a double interpretation of the Scriptures, so that after the first one, namely, a reading of the history . . . he might himself disclose both the allegorical and anagogical sense. . . . Often we examine the literal surface by busily considering what it contains that is allegorically congruent with the mysteries of Christ, and with the state of the Catholic Church, and with the censure of a person's morals.[3]

Although it is not clear here, a little further on there is an explicit reference to tropology: "Up to this point we have dealt succinctly with anointing, drawing on an allegorical explanation. But we have also approached it tropologically, that is to say, according to the rules of moral understanding." Thus, it is with Bede that "the established terms for what comes after *historia* or *littera* will be: *allegoria, tropologia, anagoge (anagogia).*"[4]

To St. Bede the historical or literal meaning is the common-sense narrative meaning of events in their natural order. Any of the historical events of the Old Testament can be taken as literal. But they can also be freely interpreted figuratively or symbolically to refer to the sacraments of the Church or to the reality of Christ. So water is taken whenever it occurs to symbolize baptism; and the vanquishing of enemies, such as Pharaoh, prefigures Christ's conquest of the devil, etc. The third sense, the moral, is revealed either denotatively (e.g., "Thou shalt not kill") or connotatively (e.g., "At all times, dress in white and keep your head well-scented" Eccl. 9:8; which means let all your acts be pure with a heart filled with love). Finally, the anagogical meaning must lead to what is higher, in this life or to what is of future glory in the next: such as Heavenly consolations and rewards, or judgement and eternal blessedness in the age to come. In every case the scriptures were to be read with a certain alertness and readiness to find lessons about Christ and his Church in everything and to apply them to personal virtue and holiness. St. Bede is the perfect example and fount of what was to follow.

After Bede the traditional form of the four senses was fairly well established. And by the time we come to Ss. Bernard of Clairvaux,

---

3. In *Sam.*, Bk. 2 cp. 2; quoted in de Lubac, vol. I, p. 93.
4. de Lubac, vol. II, p. 37.

Thomas Aquinas, and Bonaventure, we find the practice to be universal for scriptural exegesis. St. Bernard's sermons on *The Song of Songs* summarize his mystical theology. Like Origen and Augustine, Bernard allegorically interprets the bond between the Divine Word and the individual soul as a spiritual marriage between the Heavenly Bridegroom and the earthly bride. Commenting on the words, "Let him kiss me with the kiss of his mouth," Bernard compares kissing Christ's feet, hand, and mouth with the purgative, illuminative, and unitive way. He says, "these kisses were given to the feet, the hand and the mouth, in that order. The first is the sign of genuine conversion of life, the second is accorded to those making progress, the third is the experience of only a few of the more perfect." For St. Bernard, the Bridegroom will reveal himself only to one who is proved worthy by intense devotion, vehement desire and sweetest affection.

> This happens when the mind is enraptured by the unutterable sweetness of the Word, so that it withdraws, or rather is transported, and escapes from itself to enjoy the Word. The soul is affected in one way when it is made fruitful by the Word, in another when it enjoys the Word: in the one it is considering the needs of its neighbour; in the other it is allured by the sweetness of the Word. . . . But when does this happen and for how long? It is sweet intercourse, but lasts a short time and is experienced rarely! This is what I spoke of before, when I said that the final reason for the soul to seek the Word was to enjoy him in bliss.[5]

Here we find that basic principle of medieval exegesis, *viz.* that one's hermeneutic understanding of the sacred text is incomplete unless it leads one to contemplation and union with the Divine.

St Thomas, the great systematizer, clarifies and explains the four senses, albeit in an allegorical way:

> That meaning, whereby things signified by words have themselves also a meaning, is called the spiritual sense, which is based on the literal, and presupposes it. Now this spiritual sense has a threefold division. For as the Apostle says (Heb. 10:1) the Old Law is a figure

---

5. Sermon 85:13.

14

of the New Law, and Dionysius says the New Law itself is a figure of future glory.... Therefore, so far as the things of the Old Law signify the things of the New Law, there is the allegorical sense. But so far as the things done in Christ, or so far as the things which signify Christ, are types of what we ought to do, there is the moral sense. But so far as they signify what relates to eternal glory, there is the anagogical sense.[6]

Notice here that Thomas makes the literal sense foundational for the others. In so doing he carries on the tradition of the four senses but also restrains them from becoming arbitrary or fanciful.

With St. Bonaventure spiritual interpretation reaches its summit and gains its justification. In his comment on the prophetic words of Ecclesiasticus 24:12, "he who has created me has rested in my tent," he states:

According to the literal understanding, it applies to the Virgin Mary, in whose tabernacle the Lord rested bodily. According to the allegorical, it applies to the Church Militant, in whose tabernacle the Lord rests sacramentally. According to the moral, it applies to the faithful soul, in whose tabernacle the Lord rests spiritually. According to the anagogic understanding, it applies to the Heavenly court, in whose tabernacle he rests sempiternally.[7]

Bonaventure married his metaphysics of emanation, exemplarity, and return to the four senses: indeed, to all that he was to write. In his *On the Six Days* he says. "Any person who is unable to consider how things originate, how they are led back to their end, and how God shines forth in them, is incapable of achieving true understanding."[8] All things emanate from God and, therefore, bear the stamp or vestige of the Logos, through whom all things come to have their nature or identity. The world contains the Logos, as it were, quasi-sacramentally. Everything is that which God speaks it to be. Within creation lies a wealth of pellucid and luminous symbols whose prose and imagery reflect their dependence, to their very depths, upon the Eternal which sustains and expresses them. Because nothing has

6. *Summa Theol.* I. Q.1, art. 10.
7. Quoted in de Lubac, vol. II, p. 198.
8. *Hex.* 3.2 (v. 343).

anything of itself except it is received from God, everything receives proportionally some trace of his image according to its limited capacity. This capacity of embodying something of God's self-expression, in a limited way, must surely include everything literally contained in scripture as well, so that through discerning their figures one may ultimately be lead back to the mystical.

It is the universal analogy of being—the proportional likeness of the created to the Creator—that makes this possible. Insofar as all things receive their being from him, they correspond to him in a proportionate manner, and speak of him secretly and intimately to those who are open to their mysteries. From the lowest of creatures to man made in the image of God, the whole cosmos appears as sustained, ordered, and animated by the divine analogy. Therefore, because all creation bears a trace of the Divine, every creature is an allegory, or a psalm to God. Thus, St. Bonaventure has given us a profound and all-embracing metaphysics for the four senses.

Clearly one cannot detect during the High Middle Ages any notion of that critical sense which moderns apply to history. On the contrary, it was always based upon an objective and realist sense of events as foundational for its spiritual trajectory. In the words of de Lubac:

> For, except in certain rather rare cases, the exegesis that we are studying was not a specialised exegesis; it was not an auxiliary science of theology: it was theology itself—and even more that theology, if the signification of the word is extended as far as spirituality. Thus, if Scripture was a tower, its foundation was history, but its summit or head was the spiritual sense.[9]

For history was never enough to contain the mystery; above it hovered the Spirit of God. The whole of history pointed towards Christ and his kingdom; and exegesis had to follow this pattern within the individual reader as well. Christ is the meaning of history and the fulfilment of scripture: interpretation remains in darkness until his light is revealed to the believer. At the end of the process was mystical contemplation: and Christ was its beacon and its summit. Christian ecstasy was the consummation of a process, which began with the let-

---

9. de Lubac, vol. II, p. 77.

ter of the holy text, but which led the believer by degrees to the eternal where all utterance is struck dumb in simple adoration before one's God.

The Rise and Assumptions of Historical Criticism

The Enlightenment effected a transition from a world view that rested upon the authority of Revelation to one erected upon the principles of reason alone. This transition was encouraged by that general optimism stimulated by the perceived accomplishments of science and philosophy, especially those of Newton and Kant. Its influence entered theology at various levels such as doctrine, sacred history and moral and spiritual development. Some Enlightenment thinkers went so far as to collapse the distinction between religion and morality, in effect reducing theology to ethics. That way there could be no conflict between science and religion, but no distinctive claims on behalf of religion either.

Johann Salamo Semler (1725–1791) is traditionally regarded as the father of historical-critical theology. A German historian and Biblical critic, he grew up in pietistic surroundings. His studies at the University of Halle brought him under the influence of the rationalism of S.J. Baumgarten. After the death of Baumgarten in 1757, Semler became the head of the theological faculty there. His ideas were extremely influential in encouraging the application of critical reason to the Bible in a manner similar to that applied to any ancient document. However, the extent to which his contemporary, Reimarus, had pushed this progressive theology threatened to undermine the moral and spiritual substance of Semler's Christianity. This seemed to rekindle the fervency of his pietist upbringing and galvanized him to inveigh against Reimarus' historicism. However, Semler's futile attempts to counter its destructive tendencies discredited him. He died without disciples.

Following on from the contributions of these pioneers in historical criticism, there was a period of expansion and refinement in techniques. Textual criticism began to develop exacting principles of analysis and classification of texts under the aegis of Lachmann, Tischendorff, and Westcott and Hortt. Their efforts became the basis for the modern attempts to recover the pristine text after various distortions and additions are corrected. David Friedrich Strauss, who in his *Das Leben Jesu* (1835) followed Reimarus in denying the historicity of miracles, the resurrection, and the cosmology of the Gospels, attempted to save the integrity of the Biblical message through his concept of myth. He affirmed that myth was capable of expressing truths that rationalistic, naturalistic assumptions could not.

However, the most enduring contribution to historical-critical method was provided by Ernst Troeltsch's essay "On Dogmatic Method in Theology" which appeared in 1898. In that essay he formulated three principles which became the basis for modern critical scholarship: (1) the principle of methodological doubt which asserted that history could only achieve probabilistic knowledge; (2) the principle of historical analogy which argued that there is no sufficient reason to assume that events in the past required explanations beyond those available in the present experience of the historian (similar events have similar causes); and (3) the principle of correlation or mutual interdependence of events which implied that all historical phenomena were causally interrelated such that the sufficient reason for any event must be discovered solely in the immediately preceding event(s). The upshot of these principles was that history ought only to be understood as a closed system of mutually interconnected events. No other source or explanation for the events of history was to be sought outside this causal chain. As such, criticism makes every event doubtful unless it can be shown to stand in a naturally occurring causal relation to other empirically supported events.

The twentieth century was a period of both advancement and growing criticism for the historical-critical approach. The earliest of these methods to arise was source criticism. This method had a long history and grew out of the increasing awareness among scholars of the literary interdependence of the Gospels, particularly the synoptic Gospels. Ever since Justin Martyr, Irenaeus, Clement of Alexandria, Origen, Tertullian, etc., it had been known that the three synoptics contained considerable material in common to the extent that there was close agreement among them of the wording of the various sayings, parables, and narratives of Jesus. They were also aware of the disagreements in wording, order, and selection of events. It was not until the fourth century, however, that Augustine endeavoured to account for these observations by arguing in his *De Consensu Evangelistarum* that Mark used and abbreviated Matthew and that Luke utilized both Matthew and Mark. His solution to the "Synoptic Problem" relied upon the accepted canonical order.

Scholars had to wait until the latter half of the eighteenth century before a synopsis appeared which presented the four Gospels in parallel columns that facilitated a ready comparison between matched texts. In 1776, J.J. Griesbach produced his *Synopsis Evangeliorum* which stimulated a number of scholars to compare the similarities and discrepancies they found in the synoptics. These scholars proposed various explanations such as the existence of an Aramaic Ur-Gospel, an early oral tradition, and sundry, common fragments or memorabilia. Griesbach's own theory was, like Augustine's, that Matthew was the first Gospel written, that Luke, used Matthew, but (unlike Augustine) that Mark utilized and condensed the other two. However, the theory could not adequately account for why Mark would want to conflate and abbreviate these Gospels. Indeed, why do Matthew and Luke seldom agree against Mark—a fact that would require a coincidental and identical alteration in the Markan material by both Matthew and Luke? Also, Mark's Greek is often inferior to that of Matthew and Luke: it is grammatically imperfect, has more colloquialisms, and contains clumsier, redundant phrases than the other two. It is difficult to imagine that Mark would deliberately spoil their more polished versions. Furthermore, Matthew and Luke generally follow Mark's order of events, but not each other's.

Because of questions such as these, Lachmann in 1835 proposed the two-source hypothesis which hypothesized that a second source known to both the evangelists (but unknown to Mark) existed. That source was dubbed 'Q'. It comprised that material which appears in both Matthew and Luke, but not in Mark, and may in fact consist of several sources. Finally, it was realized that to account for material which is unique to Matthew and unique to Luke requires the postulation of the existence 'M' and 'L' sources to which Matthew and Luke had independent access. Thus Matthew and Luke both had the same two sources in common: Mark and a collection of materials that constituted Q. In addition, each evangelist had his own material, M and L, known uniquely to Matthew and Luke respectively. In addition to these sources, all four Gospels as well as the other NT writers quoted freely from the Old Testament, particularly from the Septuagint. All these various methods build up a compendium of sources which the NT writers are supposed to have drawn upon in compiling their respective texts.

Crisis in Methodology

In this brief introduction to historical criticism, we have mentioned a number of indicators that sources have been used in the NT documents. There are several limits to source criticism, however. While it may be advantageous in interpretation to appreciate the fact that the NT writer-editors utilized sources, there is considerable dispute among scholars as to what these were, quotations from the OT notwithstanding. It has generally been supposed that Q was a single written, albeit primitive, document in the form of a collection of sayings of Jesus. However, recent investigations make this supposition that Q was written not quite as certain as was once argued. Also, there is still disagreement as to the priority of Mark. A number of scholars have revived the Griesbach hypothesis of Matthean priority primarily because of the few, but significant, agreements between Matthew and Luke against Mark in the triple tradition, i.e., where all three synoptics record a similar event or oration. The general solution has been to hypothesize that, in addition to two or three written sources (Mark, Q, plus M or L), both Matthew and Luke were also familiar with extensive oral traditions in fairly established forms. Assuming that they both used Mark and Q plus oral traditions which they held in common, it is reasonable to suppose on statistical grounds that in some instances Matthew and Luke both turned to the same oral tradition against the Markan rendering. This is possible only if the synoptic agreements against Mark are few, which they are. However, this means that the interrelationships among the Gospels are far more complex than hitherto imagined. As Stein affirms:

It also seems clear that along with Mark and the oral and written sources from which Matthew and Luke obtained their Q material, Matthew and Luke possessed other oral and written materials, which overlapped much of what they found in Mark and their Q sources and also included material not found in any of the synoptic Gospels. Although Luke 1:1–2 makes mention of such sources, it is impossible today to reconstruct them with any certainty.

Another limitation concerns subjective elements such as judgements about comparative theological development between blocks of material. To assume that a higher Christology always implies a later Christology is specious. There can be little doubt about the rather high Christology in Paul's epistles even if one limits oneself to the seven undisputed letters. Since these were all composed before c. AD 67, and, therefore, before the Gospels (according to liberal dating), their higher theology conflicts with such a presupposition. It does not follow of necessity that advanced theology implies later dating. After all, theologies of different levels of sophistication exist together today and have continued to coexist throughout Christian history. Again, and for similar reasons, differences in style, grammar, or literary sophistication between or even within texts do not necessarily imply later dating.[10]

Historical criticism comprises a family of methods which faithfully apply the fundamental axioms of Troeltsch. Whether the technique is source, form, tradition, or redaction criticism, they all attempt to practice the principle of methodological doubt, the principle of analogy, and the principle of correlation. In so doing they bring a sceptical and rationalist pre-understanding to the scriptures which sets the agenda for what the sundry methods eventually produce. In theology as in the sciences, one's world view generates the method and the method generates the results and the results, in turn, confirm one's view of the world. It has been amply demonstrated that a method cannot prove a theory true (only confirm a particular hypothesis) and it cannot prove a theory false (only falsify a partic-

10. See Clayton Howard Ford, *Who Really Wrote the Bible?* (Mustang, Oklahoma: Tate Publishing, 2009).

ular hypothesis.) No amount of anomalies will collapse the historical-critical paradigm. One simply chooses to disregard it.

We have seen that none of the historical-critical methods produces "assured results." They produce the same inconsistencies and discontinuities that chaos theory shows is a feature of nonlinear systems. For, although the rationalism of its methodology endeavours to derive linear principles of a logical form, this does not transpire in practice. At the very point where a mind interacts with the data, there is the source for nonlinearity and creativity (chaos). Nothing in the data can, in advance, determine in a linear fashion the opinions and fancies that a scholarly mind derives there from. These presuppositions only function, like a group of commandments, to circumscribe the perimeters of the field of action. Within that field lies an infinite freedom for creative invention and for a kaleidoscopic variety of opinions. Indeed, Gödel's incompleteness theorem has proven that a set of axioms is not adequate to prove all the theorems belonging to the formal system they are intended to cover. And the Löwenheim-Skolem theorem has proven that from a given set of axioms the number of possible theories that can be generated within a formal system is indeterminate.[11] Axioms can neither prove nor delimit all the possible interpretations or deductions that can be derived from them. If this is the case with logico-mathematical systems, how much more is it with regard to less rigorous methods? *The presuppositions of the historical-critical method cannot delimit its conclusions, nor can they guarantee truth.*

Clearly these methodologies do not come alone, but bring with them various presuppositions—theological or otherwise. Perhaps the most destructive is the quite arbitrary doctrine of *sola Scriptura* which, of course, is not a teaching of scripture.[12] This sixteenth century presupposition has continued to be a restrictive influence upon exegetes which has kept them from acknowledging the documen-

11. Morris Kline, *Mathematics: The Loss of Certainty.* (Oxford: Oxford University Press, 1982), p. 271.

12. That the Scriptures are not all-inclusive by themselves, see: Mk. 4:33; 6:34; Jn. 16:12; 20:30; 21:25; Acts 1: 2–3; 1 Cor. 11:2; 1 Thess. 2:13; 2 Thess. 2:15, 3:6; 1 Tim. 3:15; 2 Tim. 1:13–14; 2:2. Col. 1:18, 24; Eph. 5:23.

tary evidence. It must be kept in mind that the historical-critical method originated from a liberal German-Protestant base which refused to include the evidence of Tradition. Scripture alone was to be the object of investigation: Tradition was not allowed to influence that process. To consider such evidence was considered an infringement of scientific freedom, as though facts must never be allowed to get in the way of theories. Yet the whole point of science is to include *all* the empirical evidence, especially documentary evidence. Rather than being a constraint on science, evidence is its very *sine qua non*!

The most severe difficulty, however, comes from what is known as the halting problem, *viz.*: is there a methodical procedure which will demonstrate that another such procedure will arrive at a valid result? Given that historical-critical methods often generate such different and inconsistent results, how does one logically select that method which *one knows* will produce the desired (true) result? A family of theorems by the logicians Church, Turing and Chaitin has proven that no such step-by-step procedure (algorithm) can exist that will decide the outcome of another. This applies directly to those methods we have been discussing, where strings of text are compared to others. Such comparisons can be effectively carried out by a computer programmed to collate and match sequences of text to determine order and relationship. However, any programme designed to determine the validity of the results produced by the first programme would be recursive, causing it to loop forever. It is, therefore, *impossible methodologically* to show that any one of these critical methods, *by itself*, will ever arrive at a conclusive solution to such problems as, for example: what are the written or oral sources behind the Gospels, in what order were they written, or how they were edited, etc. This is devastating for those effectively computable procedures which belong to what is called "higher criticism."[13]

---

13. For example, source criticism presupposes at least eight different theories proposing every permutation of order of the Synoptic Gospels, some with a hypothetical written source (Q), and some with a hypothetical oral source (Jerusalem Catechism). Because the methodical and mechanical comparisons of strings of text by source criticism can be effectively accomplished by a computer, they become

Thus, historical criticism suffers as a method because it is incapable of proving anything true and is incapable of being falsified. It cannot demonstrate that it has greater approximation to the truth for it is not open to any truth outside its limited paradigm. Neither is it reliable because it produces inconsistent results; and if it is unreliable it cannot be a valid method. It cannot even achieve referentiality—not for Q, not for the oral tradition, not for the "historical Jesus." And it is ultimately incapable of testing its historical assumptions. The most historical criticism can do is to confirm that to which it already subscribes. The most it can accomplish is the confirmation of a world view, that which may be false, and, at the same time, the demonstration that rival paradigms are inconclusive though they may be true. It maintains the status quo. The historical method essentially safeguards one's own position be it liberal (Bultmann, Bornkamm, Marxsen, Perrin, Käsemann) or conservative (Osborne, Marshall, Travis, Smalley, Wenham). Paradigms are chosen, not proven. The method simply functions to reinforce one's chosen paradigm.[14]

Undoubtedly, to argue for a closed, causal history is becoming harder and harder. Not only is this paradigm positivistic, materialistic, and deterministic, but it is woefully dated. It has been contradicted by chaos theory, by quantum physics, by morphic resonance, and by information theory. It is contradicted by chaos theory because of the sensitivity of nonlinear systems, such as the weather,

---

subject to these theorems, and thus remain undecidable. Moreover, to attempt to use one method to prove another can only lead to an infinite regression of hierarchies of methods. Apart from not heeding the objective documentary evidence, which they disclaim, the higher critics cannot specify the method whereby one could proceed to falsify their hypotheses—unlike the physical sciences.

14. It is just and prudent to disassociate the historical critics from mainstream historians. The latter by far are much more favorable to the historical accuracy of the Gospels. Not only do the majority (80%) accept the broad outlines of the events in the life of Jesus, but they also concur that from the very beginning the *primary sources show* that the followers of Jesus *believed* him to have risen from the dead and to have acknowledged him as the Son of God. For a comprehensive overview of this and an excellent bibliography of the mainstream see: John Dickson, *Jesus: A Short Life* (Oxford: Lion Hudson, 2008).

human society, the economy, and people's brains, to minute pertur-
bations, and because of the inherent unpredictability of nonlinear
systems. In quantum physics there has been an acceptance of
Heisenberg's principle of indeterminacy and an abandonment of
the principle of local causes, while the historical-critics still inhabit
a Newtonian, mechanistic universe. The theory of morphic resonance asserts that all history is governed by information fields that
learn, evolve, and determine the development of organisms and
social institutions. And information theory has described a level of
reality that is non-material, insubstantial, invisible, and non-local-
isable. Our universe can no longer be thought to conform to the
nineteenth-century rationalist paradigm. The universe has become
more wondrous than the historical critics could possibly have imagined. They do not have the right to set such narrow strictures upon
thought.

The third quest for the historical Jesus has failed for the same reasons as the previous two: one always gets the Christ of one's faith—
or lack of it (Mt. 9:29). Given that we are so imprisoned in paradigms it is no wonder that this should be so. In fact, we could never
have come to Christ unless we were drawn by God (Jn. 6:44). There
is certainly nothing in the historical-critics' Jesus to inspire us. That
is not how it happened that we first came to our faith. We do not
know why we have been drawn with such an inexorable grace to
make such a commitment (we merit nothing); but having been thus
drawn, we can only submit to its expression. We shall not doubt the
faith given to us. We have no choice but to express it, for we do not
desire to abandon it for a moment, even when doing exegesis. Or
precisely when doing exegesis: for it is a matter of personal integrity.
We cannot stifle what has been vouchsafed to us; and we do not buy
what is defective and unreliable. Whatever world view or paradigm
we choose it must always express the nature of our faith. Even here
we are judged. But we are *not constrained to surrender* to any given
paradigm.

Return to the Four Senses
It is clear that historical criticism is not true to its object, which is a
clear violation of the methodological principle of validity: a method

of observation or examination must be conformed to the object under investigation. This merely expresses the self-evident, first criterion of judgement known as the principle of identity, *viz.*, that a thing is identical to itself. Therefore, we must correctly identify the object as it is according to its nature. If the nature of the biblical text is that it is the revelation of the mystery of the Word of God—and this is *de fide*[15]—then it transcends the merely historical sense. The historical-critical method is limited, not only for all the reasons given above, but because it does not revere the nature of the content of holy scripture, and cannot ascend to its informing mystery.

Behind this lack of reverence lies that scepticism which is fed by a deficiency of faith as Romano Guardini attests: "The proper nature of the sacred text remains excluded in the strict sense of the word as long as the appropriate attitude is lacking: faith. Whoever considers the sacred text from a merely historical point of view does not at all see in it the true and proper object."[16] The true perspective towards sacred scripture is to see it for what it is: the body of testimonies of the people of God, those who have born witness to their faith in God over the centuries. The former Cardinal Joseph Ratzinger (Benedict XVI, Emeritus) also affirms this in his *Biblical Interpretation in Crisis*:

> The first presupposition of all exegesis is that it takes the Bible as *one* book. If it does so, then it has already chosen for itself the position that is rooted in much more than the literary aspects of the text. It has recognised this literature as the product of a coherent history, and this history as the proper locus of understanding. If it wishes to be theology, it must acknowledge that the faith of the Church is precisely the sort of sympathy without which the text remains closed. It must acknowledge this faith as the hermeneutic, as the locus of understanding, which does not dogmatically force itself upon the Bible, but is the only way of letting it be itself.[17]

15. See Denzinger 1787, 1952, 2009 ff; *Dei Vebum* 11, 21; *CCC.* pp. 105–107.

16. Quoted in Ignace de Potterie, "Biblical Exegesis: A Science of Faith," in Jose Granados *et al.*, *Opening Up the Scriptures: Joseph Ratzinger and the Foundations of Biblical Interpretation* (Grand Rapids: Wm. B. Eerdmans, 2008), p.55.

17. In José Granados, et al., op. cit., p. 29.

As such the book belongs to the people, attests to their struggles, and affirms their faith in God and in the Christ.

And in the Church founded by him!—with her tradition, her liturgy, her Doctors, and her hierarchy. According to Yves Congar this tradition has four aspects: Firstly, it is the transmission of the entire mystery in a variety of forms: scripture, to be sure, but also preaching, profession of faith, sacraments and external forms of worship, customs, and rules. It also includes the content of the faith: the meanings given to the realities experienced by and handed on from the people who experienced these realities. Thirdly, this tradition of testimonies forms a system of writings, institutions, liturgy, art, customs, and hagiography, which also come from the people. Finally, the subject of this transmission is the Church, comprising the people of God, whose ethos is: "the Catholic spirit together with the living manner in which the whole apostolic deposit, whose subject is the Church, is transmitted."[18] For this reason it is tradition, not some peremptory, rationalistic-deterministic ideology that must be normative for exegesis; as Jean Danielou has affirmed: "It is quite true that contact with the Bible and tradition is always necessary. Nothing is so dangerous as to substitute for this contact any kind of theological systematization. The Bible and tradition are the regulative bases to which the theologian must always refer, on pain of making arbitrary constructions."[19]

The Bible is a witness to faith, grew up in a tradition fed by faith, and is a testimony of the people of faith. These people are the very ones that we shall hear Our Lord blessing on the Mount of Beatitudes. They are the poor, the meek, those who mourn or are persecuted, the ordinary who have believed and who have left us their testimony. "God chose those who by human standards are fools to shame the wise; he chose those who by human standards are weak to shame the strong, those who by human standards are common and contemptible—indeed those who count for nothing—to reduce to nothing all those that do count for something, so that no human being might feel boastful before God" (1 Co 1:27–29). Many

---

18. *The Meaning of Tradition*, pp. 128–9.
19. *God and the Ways of Knowing*, p. 169.

of these became the saints and Doctors, whom *the Church has declared worthy* of example and belief. In short, they are the upholders and conveyers of the tradition, of which the written canon is but a part, but who are responsible for its form and content. Tradition is a font from which scripture cannot be separated if it is to be correctly understood.

> Sacred Tradition and sacred Scripture, then, are bound closely together, and communicate one with the other. For both of them, flowing out from the same divine well-spring, come together in some fashion to form one thing, and move towards the same goal.... Hence, both Scripture and Tradition must be accepted and honoured with equal feelings of devotion and reverence.[20]

Yves Congar concurs: "If tradition or the Magisterium claimed to teach something contradicting the scriptures, it would certainly be false, and the faithful ought to reject it."[21] This is becoming increasingly recognized as many scholars have become disenchanted with the disputations, contradictions, dissent, and even heresy among contemporary theologians: theologians who are causing scandal by denying the inerrancy of this deposit of faith. How many have drifted from the faith because of them? How many have fallen into spiritual complacency or even into grave sin partly as a result of their harangues against the teachings of the Church? To what extent have these critics' undermining of the truth of divine revelation contributed to the decadent and degenerate state of Western culture? For all these reasons, there grew up in the middle of the last century a pressing desire to return to the sources to rediscover our tradition and the roots of theology. Known as *ressourcement*, it included those whom we have been quoting (Guardini, Congar, Danielou, de Lubac, Ratzinger) as well as many others such as Louis Bouyer in spirituality, and Étienne Gilson in philosophy. This movement was a powerful influence upon the Second Vatican Council, and has even spread its ideals to evangelical Protestants, where their encounter with the patristic sources has prompted them

---

20. *Dei Verbum*, II, p. 9.
21. Yves Congar, *The Meaning of Tradition*, p. 100.

to question their own doctrine of *sola Scriptura* (which had been so damaging for exegesis, as we have seen).

From this movement grew the rediscovery of the four senses, which discovery has been applauded by the *Catechism of the Catholic Church*: "The profound concordance of the four senses guarantees all its richness to the living reading of scripture in the Church." After giving examples of the senses, the *Catechism* continues: "It is the task of exegetes to work, according to these rules, towards a better understanding and explanation of the meaning of sacred scripture in order that their research may help the Church to form a firmer judgement."[22] This judgement belongs to the Church to make and must include the entire canon of scripture as she has defined it.

⊕

God addresses various individuals in their existential situation and invites them into a sacramental covenant with him. From these encounters stream the entire culture and history of the people of God, a living tradition which contains that mystery which, in transcending the literal-historical, is evoked in their collective moral convictions, their intellectual imaginings, and their intuitive intimations. This divine self-revelation is a real and vital activity of which God is the designer and the prime mover. It is neither accidental nor deterministic. Rather, it is the history of a continuous engagement between God and his people. The four senses are singularly appropriate to understanding the fourfold nature of the content of this revelation. For they alone attend to the historical, psychological, moral, and spiritual culture of the people. Therefore, to comprehend this deposit requires a similar application by the exegete who also comprises body, soul, mind, and spirit. The mystery of God and his people so beautifully expressed by the symbolism of marriage as described in the *Song of Songs*—which, from St. Paul to St. Bernard of Clairvaux, was further allegorized into the

22. *CCC*, pp. 115, 119.

spousal image of Christ and his Church—is fulfilled only when the interpreter of the sacred text is, oneself, led into this same communion. Exegesis is incomplete if it does not lead us back to the mystery of Our Lord and Exemplar, who emanates from the Father in the communion of the Holy Spirit, and from whom all things receive their form and substance.

2

The Sermon in Matthew's Gospel

W E SHALL NOW briefly consider some questions concerning St. Matthew's Gospel itself and the place of Our
Lord's sermon within it and in the rest of scripture.
When we turn to the *extra-Biblical* documentary evidence we
find unanimous agreement that Matthew, the tax collector, otherwise known as Levi, was its author. Papias (c. 60–130) writes: "Matthew collected the oracles in the Hebrew language, and each
interpreted them as best he could" (Eusebius, *Historia Ecclesiastica*:
3.39.16). Irenaeus (c.130–200) who was taught by Polycarp, a disciple
of John the Apostle, states in *Adversus Haereses* 3.1.1: "Matthew also
issued a *written* Gospel among the Hebrews in their own dialect,
[then?, while?] Peter and Paul were *preaching* at Rome, and were
laying the foundations of the Church." This period can be interpreted as being either before or during AD 60–64.[1] Origen (c.185–
254) also affirms: "Having learnt by tradition concerning the four
Gospels ... that first was written that according to Matthew, who
was once a tax-collector but afterwards an apostle of Jesus Christ,
who published it for those who from Judaism came to believe, composed as it was in the Hebrew language (letters)." (*HE* 6.25.24) Sim-

---

1. The suggested conjunctions in brackets are not in the original Greek. Irenaeus
continues: "But after their departure [death], Mark, the disciple and interpreter of
Peter, has handed down to us, also in writing, what had been preached by Peter. And
Luke also, the companion of Paul, recorded in a book the Gospel preached by him.
Afterwards, John, the disciple of the Lord, who also had leaned upon His breast, did
himself publish a Gospel during his residence at Ephesus in Asia." Also see Appendix
1, 2150. It is worth noting that a fragment 7Q5, identified by Fr. J.O. Callaghan as
being from Mk. 6:52ff., was discovered at Qumran and must be dated sometime
before the cave was sealed in AD 68. See *Biblica* 53 (1972), pp. 91–109.

31

ilar statements are to be found by Epiphanius, Cyril of Jerusalem, Jerome, Gregory of Nazianzus, Chrysostom, and Augustine, as well as in several Syrian and Coptic authorities.[2] The Greek Gospel which we now possess is, of course, a later translation, since according to Eusebius—explaining the phrase οψε δε σαββατον (after the Sabbath) in Mt. 28:1—"it has been written by *him who translated the scripture*, for the evangelist [had] delivered it in the Hebrew tongue."[3] Nevertheless, the earliest existing Greek manuscripts, which preserve the title page for the Gospel, all have as their heading some variation of Κατα Ματθαιον (according to Matthew). Thus, the objective documentary evidence clearly identifies St. Matthew as the author; that he wrote an original in a Hebrew tongue or dialect; and that this was the first Gospel to be written.

Happily, all this accords with the findings of the Pontifical Biblical Commission (see Appendix). This body was originally under the authority of the Magisterium. However, Pope Paul VI completely restructured the Commission in 1971 and attached it to the Congregation for the Doctrine of the Faith as a consultative body. As a consequence it no longer retained the binding authority it originally had. Possibly this is one reason its findings have not been adhered to by some Catholic exegetes. Nevertheless, as we saw in the last chapter, nothing contrary to this evidence has been proven; neither have the original decrees of the Biblical Commission been officially rescinded. On this question—of how we should assess the first fifty years of the Biblical Commission—Joseph Ratzinger has stated:

> We are profoundly grateful for *the openings* that Vatican II has given us as the fruit of a long struggle. But we also refuse simply to condemn what went before, but see it as a necessary part of the process of knowing, which will always challenge us anew on

2. John Wenham, *Redating, Matthew, Mark, and Luke: A Fresh Assault on the Synoptic Problem* (London: Hodder & Stoughton, 1991), pp. 117–119.

3. *On the Discrepancies of the Gospels, Ad Marinum*, Quaest. 2, quoted in Wenham, *ibid.* (italics added). While Luke's Gospel was written before Acts, and Acts ends before Paul's departure to Spain in 65–67 AD (as confirmed by the fragment of Muratori, c. AD 175, and Clement of Rome, *First Epistle to the Corinthians*, 5:7, c. AD 96), nevertheless not all scholars agree that Luke did use Matthew's (Greek) Gospel.

account of the magnitude of the Word spoken to us and of the limits of our capabilities.[4]

Questions will always remain to be answered regarding the historical placement of Matthew's *Greek* Gospel among Mark's and Luke's, and their mutual dependency. It will always be possible to consider other arrangements, structures, and specific details, without ever being able to deny "that the Greek Gospel is identical as to substance with that Gospel written in his native language by the same Apostle."[5] Thus, the reader may rest assured that the Apostolic Authority of the Gospels, universally attested to by the tradition of the Fathers, remains unscathed having withstood the many attacks levelled against it.

The Structure of Matthew and the Kingdom Motif

The Kingdom is a pre-eminent motif occurring over fifty times in Matthew and serves to structure his Gospel with narrative sections alternating with discourses. The elements comprising this kingdom motif all serve to proclaim Jesus as the embodiment and fulfilment of the kingdom of David. However, in Jesus it is given a new and divine perfection.

Matthew opens his Gospel with "the genealogy of Jesus Christ, the son of David, son of Abraham." The phrase *biblos geneseos,* which means "book of genesis," is used on only two other occasions in the Septuagint: "This is the book of the origin of Heaven and

---

4. "Exegesis and the Magisterium of the Church," in Jose Granados *et al., Opening Up the Scriptures: Joseph Ratzinger and the Foundations of Biblical Interpretation* (Grand Rapids: Wm. B. Eerdmans, 2008), p. 136. *"the openings ... as the fruit of a long struggle"* i.e., with higher criticism; *"But we also refuse simply to condemn what went before"* i.e., the first fifty years of the Biblical Commission. See also pp. 133 ff.

5. See Appendix 2152 V. A Hebrew Gospel of Matthew does exist, discovered in a fourteenth century MS titled *Evan Botham* (the Touchstone). It was attached as an appendix to a polemical work written in 1380 by Shem-Tob ben Isaac ben Shavrut, a physician residing in Aragon. It includes the entire Gospel of Matthew with critical comments interspersed throughout. The several divergences to the Greek Matthew, found in the text, indicate that ben Shavrut used an earlier Hebrew source. However, no one is in a position to determine when or why the earlier Hebrew Matthew existed, much less whether this points to an even earlier Hebrew original.

earth" (Gen. 2:4) and "This is the book of the origin of men, on the day God made Adam, he made him in the image of God" (5:1). It is not without significance that both phrases refer to creation, implying more than mere procreation, since for all the other genealogies in Genesis another construction is used. Thus with the coming of Jesus we are presented with a new beginning. The enigmatic seed that in the end would crush the head of the serpent—as was first promised to Eve in Genesis 3:15—was destined to be the scepter that would issue from the tribe of Judah (49:10), the ancestor of Jesse the father of King David (Mt. 1:5–6). He would "grow mighty in Ephratha, be renowned in Bethlehem" (Ruth 4:11, Mt. 2:5–6).

This lineage was to have a definite messianic consummation. In him YHWH would establish an everlasting royal house: "I have made my covenant with my Chosen One, sworn an oath to my servant David: I have made your dynasty firm for ever, built your throne stable age after age" (Ps. 89:3–4).[6] Isaiah 11:1–2 had also prophesied: "a shoot will spring form the stock of Jesse, a new shoot will grow from his roots. On him will rest the spirit of the LORD, the spirit of wisdom and insight, the spirit of counsel and power, the spirit of knowledge and fear of the LORD." And this Spirit visibly comes down to rest upon Jesus like a dove (Mt. 3:16–17). Here one is reminded of the creation where the Spirit of God hovered over the surface of the waters when light first illumined the world. Matthew affirms that this prophetic expectation has finally been fulfilled in Jesus whose kingdom is to transcend that of David and is to be extended over all creation and all of time: "from this time onward you will see the Son of man seated at the right hand of the Power and coming on the clouds of Heaven" (26:64).

As a consequence, this expected kingdom has been divinized and realized in Jesus who has received "all authority in Heaven and on earth" (Mt. 28:18). Matthew's Gospel culminates with Jesus' commissioning the disciples to teach and observe his commands promising to be with them always. Thus, the promises, originally covenanted by God the Father to Abraham, are mediated by the prefigured anointed Son of King David, and bestowed by him upon

6. See also 2 Sam. 7:12–16; Isa. 9:6–7; Ezek. 34:23–34; Hos. 3:5.

all those descendents of Abraham's faith who, by remaining stead-fast disciples, are made worthy to receive his blessings.

Matthew also deliberately alludes to several parallels between the life of Jesus and Moses: As with the birth of Moses a pagan king orders the slaughter of infants; like Moses the infant Jesus is pro-tected through divine intervention; both are called out of Egypt; while Moses walks through the Red Sea, Jesus walks on the Sea of Galilee; both make a spiritual retreat to the wilderness; just as Moses delivers the Law from Sinai, so Jesus delivers his first sermon from Mount Eremos; Moses feeds the children of Israel with manna and Jesus feeds the five thousand; Moses heals his people with a bronze serpent, while Jesus heals with his word; and just as Moses' face shone with a divine radiance after descending Mount Sinai (Ex. 34:29–31), so the face of Jesus "shone like the sun and his clothes became as dazzling as light" when Our Lord was transfigured upon Mount Tabor (Mt. 17:2). These and other parallels identify Jesus as the type answering to Moses' prefigurement, thus fulfilling the prophecy given to Moses in Deut. 18:15–19 that God would raise a prophet like himself: "From your own brothers I shall raise up a prophet like yourself; I shall put my words into his mouth and he will tell them everything." (See especially Acts 3:22, 7:37 where this analogy is already assumed by the early Christians.)

However, the identification of Jesus as a type of Moses is meant to imply more than the office of prophet. For Moses was also the one to lead and deliver his people. Moses had rescued the children of Israel from slavery and bondage to Pharaoh, but Jesus would save his people from sin and from the dominion of Satan: "you must name him Jesus, because he is the one who is to save his people from their sins" (Mt. 1:21). And often Jesus was described as casting out demons. Indeed, the Greek word translated "from" (*apo*) is best expressed by the conception of separation or removal from so that the meaning is that Jesus will save his people away from sin itself, from a life in bondage to sin. Combined with this further analogy to Moses, the Davidic covenant takes on a new meaning, for the law given through Moses written on tablets of stone would, through Christ, become a new law written on their hearts (Jer. 31:31–34).

Jesus is also the expected Messiah who institutes his visible kingdom on earth. This is brought out explicitly in the central pericope of Matthew 16:13–20.[7] While Jesus was at Caesarea Philippi, but before he was to make his way to Jerusalem to die, he pressed his disciples to inquire of them who they thought he was. It was Peter who finally spoke the words: "You are the Christ, the Son of the living God." That Peter is not the originator of this utterance is plain from the words of Jesus: "Blessed are you, Simon Bar-Jona! For flesh and blood has not revealed this to you, but my Father who is in Heaven." Jesus addresses Simon formally, using his family name, thereby officially sanctioning that the latter is speaking under the inspiration of God who had singled him out from among the apostles for this revelation. Jesus plainly points out that it is Peter who is the rock: "*You are Peter (Petros)*, and on this rock (*petra*) I will build my church (*ecclesia*)."[8] Jesus is the chief cornerstone (Eph. 2:20; 1 Pt. 2:6) upon which Peter the rock was grounded. Peter is the rock because God had graced him for this revelation. And that is why Jesus *will* (future) build his Church upon *this petra* by handing to Peter the "the keys to the kingdom of Heaven."[9] This is a clear allusion to "the key of the house of David" that the Davidic king of Israel would entrust to his chief steward: "I shall place the key of David's palace on his shoulder; when he opens, no one will close, when he closes, no one will open. I shall drive him like a nail into a firm place; and he will become a throne of glory for his family" (Is. 22:22–23). These keys to the kingdom were given to Peter to symbolize and to establish his authority to bind and to loose in perpetuity.

The Hebrew prophets proclaimed a future messianic kingdom

---

7. This narrative occurs in every single manuscript and translation of Matthew. In fact, Bruce Metzger, points out that the title Jesus Christ occurring in the Greek in verse 21 is directly dependent upon Peter's earlier confession. For that reason the committee of the *Greek New Testament* preferred to substitute "Jesus" in that verse. See *A Textual Commentary of the Greek New Testament*, pp. 42–43.

8. The difference in the endings of the Greek word for rock is simply because rock is feminine in Greek, but Peter is masculine. However, in the Aramaic which Jesus spoke, the word for rock was identical in both cases: "You are Cepha and upon this cepha I will build. . . ."

9. Mt. 16:19. Placing keys upon a person's shoulder had been the traditional custom for delegating authority to anyone taking over the management of a large household. Cf. Gen. 41:40–44; 43:19; 44:4; 1 Kgs. 4:5–6; 16:9; 18:3; Rev. 3:7; 19:27.

that would be national and temporal, but at the same time would be universal and eschatological. From the very beginning of Matthew, Jesus preached this kingdom as having arrived already in his Person and, while it begins as an internal spiritual dominion of Christ within the soul, it is extended through a social and visible community that already existed at the time of Christ.[10] The parables of the kingdom given by Jesus in Matthew's Gospel illustrate these themes clearly. The kingdom is like a mustard seed, a pearl, or a treasure hidden in a field. Its beginnings are small and interior, but it is so precious that one relinquishes everything for its sake. Its influence spreads so widely that many come to dwell within its compass. However, it also suffers enemies who strive to corrupt it. Nevertheless, those who oppose the kingdom will be weeded out in the end when the Church finally stands triumphant under the dominion of Christ the King.

This kingdom is to be realized in a visible, temporal Church founded upon the rock of St. Peter to whom was given the power of the keys; and that it would spread its branches to encompass many peoples. The manifestation of the kingdom as the nascent primitive Church is merely incipient in those first called to hear Our Lord's sermon. But being built upon a rock it will perdure through all time, enduring all the storms and onslaughts of worldly circumstance, never to fall.

The foregoing typologies of the Davidic King, the prophet Moses (deliverer and lawgiver), and the high priestly office of Peter, should suffice to establish the traditional attribution of the titles of Prophet, Priest, and King to Jesus. Thus, when we witness Jesus ascending and descending the Mount of Beatitudes, we shall immediately find ourselves in the presence of a figure of unearthly majesty, authority, and blessedness: one who concretizes the entire Old Testament in its context, milieu, and trajectory. It is Jesus himself who both embodies and brings the kingdom, immediately and forever. The kingdom of Christ transcends and includes all of time, yet at each moment is present in the community gathered in his name (Mt. 18:20; 28:20). Christ is the centre of this kingdom, its chief cor-

10. Mt. 6:33; 7:21; 11:12; 12:28.

nerstone, life, and principle. He is its hidden treasure, its head and its crown. As such the kingdom is both visible and invisible, consummated yet advancing, holy though imperfect. He is the Lord, "the Christ, the Son of the living God."

The Sermon within Matthew's Gospel

The Sermon on the Mount occurs within a section of Matthew designated by scholars as the Announcing of the Kingdom. In this first major discourse, Jesus radically portrays what it means to live under the reign of "the Father," to go beyond the limits of the law, to follow a different path from the world, and to become as perfect as God is. Even the prayer he teaches intimates that there is a deep communion between God's children and their Heavenly Father who cares for them so providentially. Furthermore, he reveals a profound Christology, since the perfection he requires is precisely that of the beatitudes which Jesus himself possesses perfectly. Lastly, Jesus reveals himself as the lawgiver and the world's final judge who determines the eternal destiny of every individual. Throughout it all Our Lord speaks with an authority that astonishes the crowds.

The sermon itself is well structured, as are all Our Lord's discourses. Like the rest of Matthew it is centred on the kingdom, which is mentioned throughout the discourse (5:3, 10, 19, 20; 6:10, 33; 7:21). Firstly, Jesus speaks of the nature of the people of the kingdom: their character and blessedness, their relation to the world, and their personal sufferings. They are the salt of the earth and the light of the world.

Secondly, Our Lord expounds the righteousness of the kingdom, setting forth a high standard of virtue demanded from his people by the King. This righteousness, fully in accordance with the principles set forth in the Law and the Prophets, nonetheless must exceed the righteousness of the scribes and the Pharisees—the Scriptural exegetes and religious teachers in Jesus' day. This righteousness must have the love of God at its centre and must be animated, formed, and led by this devotion. Such devotion is to be so radical as to involve complete and utter trust and abandonment to God's providential care. It is to include the love of one's neighbor without hypocrisy, stinginess, or judgement, but rather with promptitude, meekness, and generosity.

Finally, Jesus concludes with an exhortation to enter the kingdom setting out the two ways. He describes the commencement of the way, its difficulties, and how it differs from the way of the world. Our Lord warns what happens to those who are merely hearers rather than doers, contrasting their respective eternal fates.

Pope Benedict (Emeritus), sums up the role of the sermon in Matthew's Gospel in his *Jesus of Nazareth* (p. 68): "The Sermon on the Mount is the new Torah brought by Jesus . . . as the new Moses whose words constitute the definitive Torah." We have already seen that the sermon could be understood within the new covenanted Davidic kingdom that God was establishing with the new Israel. Because he also typified the Mosaic legislating and priestly leader of God's people under the covenant, Jesus was revealing the message underlying the dramatic miracles and healings which he had been performing earlier in Matthew's gospel: *viz.* that the kingly power of God was to be manifested in the activities and teaching of Jesus. As Matthew summarized it, "Jesus went throughout Galilee, teaching in their synagogues and proclaiming the good news of the kingdom and curing every disease and every sickness among the people" (Mt 4:23). The sermon closes this opening section in Matthew of the announcing of the kingdom where Jesus is portrayed as ministering in this manner. Pope Benedict further concludes that: "In the Sermon on the Mount Jesus speaks to his people, to Israel, as to the first bearer of the promise. But in giving them the new Torah, he opens them up, in order to bring to birth a great new family of God drawn from Israel and the Gentiles. Matthew wrote his Gospel for Jewish Christians and, more widely, for the Jewish world, in order to renew this great impulse that Jesus had initiated" (p. 101).

A Note on the Sermon in Luke

Luke's Gospel was originally combined with the *Acts of the Apostles* and obviously precedes it. That Acts is early can be inferred from its failure to chronicle significant events such as Nero's persecution from AD 64–68, the deaths of St James the less in 62, of St. Peter c.64, and of St. Paul c.66–67, the Jewish revolt and the flight of Christians to Pella in 66, climaxing with the prophesied fall of Jerusalem in AD 70. Also, there is no mention made either of the outcome of the trial of Paul nor of his journey to preach the Gospel in Spain. Rather the reader is left with an anticlimax.[11]

However, the Muratorian Canon gives an explanation for this abrupt ending:[12]

> The Acts of all the apostles, however, are written in one book. Luke, *to the most excellent Theophilus,* includes events *because they were done in his own presence,* as he also plainly shows *by leaving out* the *passion of Peter,* and also *the departure of Paul* from the City on his journey to Spain.

Thus, Luke included in Acts those events to which he also was a witness, not constrained to rely solely upon eyewitnesses as in his earlier Gospel. The contention of the Muratorian document is that Luke did not have to omit the death of St. Paul, even though (as the document assumes) Luke knew of it, but only his departure from Rome, because *he was still alive and was on his way to Spain* (Ro. 15:24, 28).[13] But Luke (who apparently had previously left for Philippi c. AD 62)[14] was not a witness to this.

---

11. Given the expectation of Paul's eventual death placed in the reader by Acts 9:15–16 and 21:13, the existing ending is an anticlimax. Paul's death would be the "natural" ending. See also Acts 5:41; 14:22.

12. Discovered in 1740 by Ludovico Muratori (1672–1750), scholar, historian, and antiquary, who is regarded as the father of Italian history. This fragment of eighty-five lines consists of a list of those New Testament books considered canonical at the time. It was composed in Rome and can be dated to the third quarter of 2nd cent. because of its assertion that Hermas wrote the *Shepherd* "*lately in our times* while his brother Pius, the bishop, was sitting in the chair of the church of the city of Rome" (Pope Pius I: AD 140–155).

13. "[A]fter reaching the *limits of the West* [Paul] bore witness before the rulers." Clement of Rome, *First Epistle to the Corinthians* (5:7). That Paul made it to Spain comfortably after his release, cf. Joseph Holzner, *Paul of Tarsus* (London: Sceptre, 2008), p. 515f. Paul was rearrested and sentenced to death c. 66–67. Nero committed suicide in the summer of AD 68.

14. Ahead of Epaphroditus—Luke is not mentioned among those who send their greetings to the Philippians. Was he on his way to visit Theophilus? Did he have the MS of Acts with him? Luke, who had accompanied Paul to Rome (Acts

This explanation provides a clear alternative to the claim, made by the critics, that St. Luke for reasons of effect intentionally fabricated his ending to a historical account (*diegesis*). They maintain, without any evidence, that Luke wanted to end with Paul triumphantly preaching in Rome and so, even though he remained with him this time (2 Tim. 4:11), Luke (Paul's legal adviser)[15] suppressed information about the proceedings of Paul's second trial and even his death (2 Tim. 4:6). But why not end with the greatest sacrifice one can make for the Gospel: martyrdom? Why would St. Luke deprive St. Paul's life's testimony of this victorious crown (vv. 4:6–8, 18)? What is more, this was allegedly done in a posthumous report specifically dedicated to Luke's eminent contemporary, Theophilus, for whom Luke-Acts was written! The simplest and most plausible conclusion is that Luke had already completed Acts before Paul went to Spain, and even before his first trial (see 2 Tim. 4:16).

Moreover, in Eusebius we also have the testimony of Clement of Alexandria (c. 150–215) regarding the gospels that: "Clement . . . says that those which contain the genealogies [i.e., Matthew and Luke] were written first." Then Clement goes on to say: "When *Peter had proclaimed the word publicly at Rome* . . . as there were a great number present, they requested Mark . . . to reduce these things to writing, and that after composing the gospel he gave it to those who requested it of him" (6.14.5,6). Given that there is no hard evidence to support the critics' claim of a late date for Luke-Acts, and since the only objections to an early date for Luke's Gospel result from the suppositions generated by an unprovable and intrinsically invalid methodology—as shown in the previous chapter—there is no reason not to accept the testimony of tradition. As it was with the evidence for the Gospel of Matthew, so this testimony is also in accordance with the findings of the Pontifical Biblical council (Appendix 2160 VI, 2161 VII).

27:1; 28:16) and visited him during his first imprisonment (Col. 4:14; Philemon 1:24), later returned to visit Paul when he was reincarcerated (2 Tim. 4:11). Cf. Holzner, ibid., pp. 506, 515, 521.

15. "The third book of the Gospel, that according to Luke, was compiled in his own name on Paul's authority by Luke the physician, when *after Christ's ascension Paul had taken him to be with him like a legal expert.*" Muratorian Canon.

Luke attests in his Gospel that he relied on sources that he describes as "eyewitnesses and ministers of the word" (1:2). And according to Luke (6:13–16), Matthew was there at the sermon along with the other apostles. This seems to indicate that Matthew's account and Luke's more truncated version are of the same sermon. But, of course, the scholars are divided. Nevertheless, both Luke and Matthew confirm that Jesus went into nearby Capernaum after he finished his sermon to heal the centurion. One need only visit the area only two kilometers west of Capernaum to see for oneself that the traditional mount upon which the sermon was delivered has a level place about halfway down the mountain—see the beginning of the next chapter—exactly as Luke described in the original Greek. This fact should allay any supposition about Luke's having provided us with a different "Sermon on the Plain."

Luke's sermon begins with the beatitudes and the woes. In the four beatitudes the poor are identified as a particular people more than in Matthew where they are described as poor in spirit. Therefore, those who weep and hunger are not to be regarded as distinct groups, but are the same people of God who, in Luke's last beatitude, rejoice because they are identified with the prophets. It is also to be observed here that the woes pronounced upon those who are rich or who are laughing now reflect the same reversals that are given by Mary in her Magnificat. As such, these woes emphasize that the proud-hearted, the rich, and the mighty are presently under a judgement that has already commenced with the coming of Jesus. It follows by contrast that the people of God do also immediately share in the blessings of the kingdom.

Luke's presentation of the Lord's Prayer is not located in the sermon, but has later been linked to a parable that is unique to his Gospel. At first sight, Luke's phrasing seems to reflect a more organic and practical petition than the more spiritualized form in Matthew. Its linkage with the parable of the importunate friend at midnight is meant to emphasize the point that prayer must be persistent and that God is always ready to give. Yet this is followed immediately by the "ask, seek, and knock" passage, which in Matthew is separated from the prayer and seems to be without any context, but in Luke is illustrated by the exaggerated imagery of a wicked parent giving a snake instead of the requested fish, or a scorpion instead of an egg. "If you then, evil as you are, know how to give your children what is good, how much more will the Heavenly Father give the Holy Spirit to those who ask him!" (11:13). The addition of "Holy Spirit" clarifies the more general "good things" as recorded in Matthew. Therefore, the context that Luke gives to the Lord's Prayer shows that he is, like Matthew, aware of its more elevated meaning.

As in Matthew, throughout Luke's presentation of the sermon we are reminded of what it means to be a good disciple. "The good man out of the good treasure of his heart produces good." It is one's inner nature that determines the quality and kind of fruit that one's life will yield. This is made explicit at the end: "For the words of the mouth flow out of what fills the heart." Like Matthew, Luke emphasizes sincerity of heart, but in more specific and realistic language.

These few examples should serve to illustrate that there is no fundamental difference in the message in Luke's and Matthew's presentation of the Sermon on the Mount. There are only distinctions in style that are more evidential of the influence of their different personalities and cultural backgrounds—Luke the Macedonian physician and Matthew the Jewish tax gatherer. Yet this need not weigh upon our reading of the sermon, however, because in any case we shall follow the canonical interpretation contained in our first principle: we regard all scripture as inspired by God. Therefore, we are free to utilize Luke to illuminate our understanding, even for those verses of St. Matthew's account which are found scattered in other parts of St. Luke's Gospel.

⊕

Implicit in all these themes, taken from Matthew's Gospel as a whole and from the sermon in particular, are those four senses of scripture we have explored previously. Against the background of a literal history and erected upon that narrative, were the various typological associations which have been allegorically applied to Jesus by St. Matthew. However, these four senses are apparent not only in the typologies we have encountered, but in all the parables of Jesus as well. We have also noted the ethical dimension of the sermon. However, it is insufficient and superficial to rest upon this tropological sense merely. Rather, in order to do justice to all that Matthew (and Our Lord) intends, a conscientious and thorough exegesis must rise to the Christological, ecclesial, and eschatological dimensions as well. Furthermore, threaded through all these is the appeal to enter into the kingdom spiritually. The kingdom of Heaven must never be received as an external imposition of rules and directives that the citizen must stoically struggle to obey. Such legalism would stultify its life-giving truth. On the contrary, Christ's reign is an urgent and vital reality, inscribed in the heart, which can only be made actual through a profound and real identification with Jesus' Person. This latter conformation, of course, belongs to the fourth—anagogical—sense. Therefore, it is a natural and wholly justified exhortation made by the Church for "exegetes to work, according to these rules."[16]

16. *CCC*, 119.

PART TWO
The Sermon on the Mount

3

Prologue: The Blessed Virtues

5 ¹Seeing the crowds, he went onto the mountain. And when he
was seated his disciples came to him. ²Then he began to speak.
This is what he taught them:

A T THE FOOTHILLS of the Golan Heights, just west of the cities of Capernaum and Chorazin, lie several verdant hills.
One of these, Mount Eremos, was considered since the
fourth century to be the traditional site of Our Lord's sermon.
Today halfway up the hill on a wide level place there stands the
beautiful Church of the Beatitudes run by the Franciscan Sisters. It
overlooks the plain of Genessaret that borders the western shore of
the Sea of Galilee. Lonely mountains like these were traditionally
sacred places in the ancient world. We recall Abraham's offering of
Isaac on one of the mountains of Moriah, Moses ascending Mount
Horeb to receive the Ten Commandments, and Elijah upon Carmel
defeating the prophets of Baal. Upon this rock-strewn mount Jesus,
having spent the night in prayer, collected his disciples and then
descended to address the expectant crowds gathered below. It was
late spring or early summer, Passover having passed.[1] Seated upon a
rock among the anemones and grass, he lifted his eyes upon his disciples: those who would follow him. And Wisdom spoke.

1. For the background to this paragraph see Luke 6:12–17. It is not certain
whether it was the first or second Passover (Jn. 2:12–13) of Our Lord's ministry
which is alluded to in some manuscripts of Luke 6:1 ("on the second Sabbath after
the first Pesach"). It was probably late morning by the time the crowds had gathered.

³ How blessed are the poor in spirit: the kingdom of Heaven is theirs. ⁴ Blessed are the gentle: they shall have the earth as inheritance. ⁵ Blessed are those who mourn: they shall be comforted. ⁶ Blessed are those who hunger and thirst for uprightness: they shall have their fill. ⁷ Blessed are the merciful: they shall have mercy shown them. ⁸ Blessed are the pure in heart: they shall see God. ⁹ Blessed are the peacemakers: they shall be recognised as children of God. ¹⁰ Blessed are those who are persecuted in the cause of uprightness: the kingdom of Heaven is theirs. ¹¹ Blessed are you when people abuse you and persecute you and speak all kinds of calumny against you falsely on my account. ¹² Rejoice and be glad, for your reward will be great in Heaven; this is how they persecuted the prophets before you.

The word translated "blessed" can also mean fortunate or happy. It occurs throughout the Wisdom literature of Sirach, Psalms and Proverbs where it attributes a spiritual quality or state to those who delight in the law, whose sins are forgiven, who fear God, or trust in him and so receive consolation from him. Typically these formulae consist of: an ascription of blessedness, a description of the one so blessed, and the reason for this privilege. However, Jesus calls blessed those who, by following his example, become worthy to inherit his Father's kingdom. Our Lord's beatitudes follow an ascending spiral bringing the blessed more securely under God's reign and to friendship with Jesus himself.

How blessed are the poor in spirit: the kingdom of Heaven is theirs. Where Matthew has "poor in spirit," Luke has "blessed are you poor." This should cause no difficulty since behind the (unusual) use of the Greek *ptochoi* (poor), first mentioned by Isaiah 61:1 in the Septuagint, stands the Hebrew *anawim* in the Masoretic text.[2] Matthew, the Jew, is bringing out the spiritual sense of *anawim*, while

2. The Septuagint was the Greek translation of the Hebrew Old Testament made in the third and second centuries BC. It was used by the early Christians and was quoted by all the writers of the NT. The Masoretic text is the traditional Hebrew Bible. Although the Hebrew canon was not finally established until the Masorah (Hebrew scholars) worked on it between 600 and AD 900, nevertheless discoveries of the Dead Sea Scrolls have vindicated its textual accuracy.

Luke, the physician, is emphasizing the material meaning of *ptochoi*. Both interpretations are correct for the *anawim* traditionally were the poor, afflicted, oppressed, wretched, and meek who were particularly deserving of God's favor. In Zephaniah they are the faithful remnant among the children of Israel who, though shunned by the world, continue to remain steadfast (3:12, 14–20). They are pictured as outcast, shamed, and impoverished, yet awaiting deliverance. This deliverance would only come about through Israel via her Messiah who would assemble all the nations before God's holy mountain to accept the divine law (Is. 2:2–4).

However, the message from Our Lord is that the Kingdom of Heaven already belongs to those who have heeded his call and follow him. Both Matthew and Luke have described how Jesus, having just called his disciples, addressed his words to them—but also within the hearing of the crowd. Everything begins with God whose elective purpose by its very nature elicits that poverty of spirit that brings those who truly respond under the reign of Heaven. This is best expressed by the parable of the treasure in the field (Mt. 13:44). Just as the treasure lay hidden all the while in the field and the need to obtain the field did not exist until the find was made, so when the call of God is felt, one's essential poverty and wretchedness is recognized and everything is sacrificed to secure his riches.

Blessed are those who mourn: they shall be comforted.[3] Those who mourn in the Old Testament are either those who yearn for release from their own personal misery (Ps. 43:2; 88:9); or those who intercede for the deliverance of their people in exile (Ezr. 10:6; Tb. 13:14; Is. 61:2; Ezk. 9:4). Likewise in perceiving our own spiritual and moral deficiency and that of our world that oppresses so, we also

---

3. We have not followed the order of the New Jerusalem Bible here, preferring the order of the majority of earlier Greek manuscripts. Bruce Metzger says: "If verses 3 and 5 had originally stood together, with their rhetorical antithesis of Heaven and earth, it is unlikely that any scribe would have thrust verse 4 between them. On the other hand, as early as the second century copyists reversed the order of the two beatitudes so as to produce such an antithesis and to bring πτοχοι (poor) and πραιες (meek) into closer connection." (*A Textual Commentary of the Greek New Testament*, United Bible Societies, 1971, p. 12.)

mourn humanity's alienation from God. Although we, the poor in
the Lord, find ourselves "strangers in a strange land"—shocked by
its brutality, frustrated by its blindness, disconcerted by its ava-
rice—nevertheless we, though called apart (*ecclesia*), share a bond
with all the peoples of the world. We are fallen too; and we cannot
receive salvation alone. That we are "our brother's keeper" spurs us
dutifully to petition and to offer sacrifices for others' deliverance
also, for we are all of a piece.

But how shall we who mourn be comforted; and whence will it
come? Of all the examples of those who mourn in the Bible, surely
the most poignant is that of Job whose sufferings involved the loss
of everything he possessed and all whom he loved, so that he was
reduced to sitting on ashes, scraping his sores with a potsherd, cursing the day he was born. Throughout it all Job maintains his innocence against those who accusingly carp at him. Yet he is unable to
find solace in anything except faith: "I know that I have a living
Defender and that he will rise up last, on the dust of the earth. After
my awakening, he will set me close to him, and from my flesh I shall
look on God" (v.19:22). In the end the Creator and Lord of all enters
the drama proclaiming his immensity, power, and majesty. Job
humbled, repents confessing: "Before, by my ear I heard of thee, but
now my eye sees thee" (42:5). Then the Lord restores to Job double
of what he had before, including an incredibly long life. The answer
to Job, who personifies the oppressed people of God, lies in his
assurance of God's all-encompassing providence.

As in the book of Job, so in Isaiah, God's sovereignty over the
nations and over history is proclaimed (cf. ch. 40). The poor in
spirit, who await the Lord and so mourn but hope in him still, can
take comfort in the promises of God. "Comfort, comfort my people, says your God, speak tenderly to Jerusalem, and cry to her that
her warfare is ended, that her iniquity is pardoned, that she has
received from the Lord's hand double for her sins" (vs. 1–2). But this
comfort is more tangible for the community Jesus called to be his
disciples. Their hope is answered in the Person of Jesus himself who
is "our hope of glory" (Col. 1:27). Isaiah's chapter ends with: "But
they who hope in the Lord shall regain their strength, they will
sprout wings like eagles. . . ." Indeed, they shall laugh (Lk. 6:21).

Blessed are the gentle: they shall have the earth as inheritance. Matthew's use of the word *praeis* here is the usual translation of *anawim* which gives a definite progression over *ptochoi* used before: for the disciple having placed all trust in God's majesty, now bows before him in meekness and serenity. The disciple is blessed with a quiet confidence in God's providence, and gentleness pervades the earth. This still, quiet confidence in God is the source of meekness, all presumption having passed. "We are all beggars before God," St. Francis used to say. We are but his lowly creatures; dependent upon him for all that we have been given and ever will receive. And because only good things come from God, we can now receive with both joy and serenity all that Our Lord wills to give. Consolation and chastisement are all the same to us: they are from Our Lord who would even give us the earth as our inheritance.

The word *eretz* in Hebrew can mean land or earth. However, it is in the sense of "land" that the term is used four times in Psalm 37: "The meek (*anawim*) shall inherit the land" and "For such as are blessed of him shall inherit the land" (vs. 11, 22; cf. 29, 34). Now when it is remembered that this (promised) land later became a figure of the future kingdom which is to be possessed by God's faithful—of which the New Jerusalem was to be its signal city—then the meaning of this beatitude becomes clearer. Jesus has merged verses 11 and 22 pledging, to those who follow his example of humility, an everlasting inheritance. Though "being in the form of God, he emptied himself" and became like the *anawim*, his servants in humility and in suffering. Jesus, though "meek and humble of heart," (Mt. 11:29) has received complete authority to promise this. So if the humble *anawim* are to inherit the land, how much more so the Lamb of God who patiently endured all? For to him "all authority in Heaven and earth has been given" (Mt. 28:18). Therefore, he has the authority to commission those who follow him to share his ministry and to make disciples of all nations. Moreover, on the day of judgement they will hear the words: "Come, you *who my Father has blessed, take as your inheritance the kingdom* prepared for you since the foundation of the world" (Mt. 25:34).

Blessed are those who hunger and thirst for uprightness: they shall have their fill. Note that Luke 6:21 omits *and thirst for uprightness.* This variation maintains the respective spiritual and material interpretations of the evangelists noted above. It may also explain why Luke did not include the four more spiritual beatitudes (the gentle, the merciful, the pure in heart, and the peacemakers) instead pronouncing woes upon those who contrast with his first four. While Matthew emphasizes the Kingdom of Heaven fulfilled in Christ, Luke, the historian, traces its development in history.[4] Thus, it is no surprise that Matthew should continue with the same group who are awaiting their redemption.

The word for righteousness, justice (*tsedekah*) is used in the OT to express both God's faithfulness to his covenant and Israel's obedient response. Our Lord, who is the substance of all that is good, is himself the source and foundation of all righteousness; so that in order to be in a right relationship with God it is necessary that one conform to his law. "It is not anyone who says to me, 'Lord, Lord,' who will enter the kingdom of Heaven, but the one who does the will of my Father in Heaven" (Mt. 7:21). Therefore, to hunger and thirst for righteousness is to yearn for the consummation of God's righteous Kingdom. However, though the poor and hungry are always with us and rightly deserve our charity, it is in vain, not to mention anachronistic, to seek in sacred scripture some political programme of economic reversal. Rather, the message of the beatitudes is that, from the perspective of Heaven, their condition is actually preferable to the materially rich who do not feel the need for God and, therefore, do not seek him. They who seek shall find, and in finding they will be satisfied.

Blessed are the merciful: they shall have mercy shown them. The Old Testament repeatedly portrays God as merciful in pardoning the guilty and in extending help to those in need. Moreover, Israel is exhorted to imitate God's mercy. Mercy (*eleesa*), both as pardon and help, is an attribute of Jesus also. Five times the refrain *Kyrie eleison* issues from the mouths of those in dire need: three from the

---

4. Luke-Acts was once a single piece of work.

blind (Mt. 9:27; 20:30–31), from the Canaanite woman on behalf of her possessed daughter (15:22), and from the father of the demoniac (17:15). In each instance Jesus shows mercy through healing or deliverance. This theme continues throughout Matthew's Gospel where it is those who are merciful who have mercy shown to them.[5] For example, when Peter asks the Lord how many times must one forgive one's brother—whether it should be seven times. Jesus answers seventy-seven times. Then he proceeds to tell the parable about the unforgiving servant who is forgiven an unredeemable debt of 10,000 talents (one talent being about 6000 days' wages), while he refused to forgive a debt of 100 denarii (about 100 days' wages). His punishment of being thrown into debtors' prison only emphasizes his guilt in refusing to show mercy: "And that is how my Heavenly Father will deal with you unless you each forgive your brother from your heart" (18:35). As we forgive, so we are forgiven.

Blessed are the pure in heart: they shall see God.

> Who shall go up to the mountain of the LORD?
> Who shall stand in his holy place?
> The clean of hands and pure of heart,
>   whose heart is not set on vanities,
>   who does not swear an oath in order to deceive.
> Such a one will receive a blessing from the LORD,
>   saving justice from the God of his salvation. (Ps. 24:3–5)

Nothing unclean or unholy can stand before the Holy One of Israel. We recall how Moses was only allowed to see God's back lest he die, how Israel had to separate herself from the ungodly nations, how she had to purge herself of idols, how the Holy of Holies was reserved for consecrated priests who could enter only on the Day of Atonement, and how Israel had to endure some seventy years in exile before being allowed entry once again into the Holy Land. The heart, which is the centre of the will and the fountain of one's dispositions, feelings, and thoughts, also must be singly devoted to God (Mt. 15:18–19; 22:37). For in the end the blessed vision of God

---

5. See 6:12, 14–15; 18:21–35; 25:31–40.

shall overwhelm us. His holiness shall transform us so that we shall be rendered as incapable of sin as is God himself. "You shall be perfect as your Heavenly Father is perfect" (Mt. 5:48). It would, therefore, be immoral, unprincipled, and unjust of the Holy One to show his Glory to the unclean who could not stand before him; or to the finally impenitent who would have to be forcibly purified against their will. Now God knows this and respects the free will that he willed to give our natures. It is from love that God remains hidden: he justly and mercifully reserves the Heavenly vision of himself only for those who have shown themselves willing to be purified of all that is unseemly in their hearts.

Blessed are the peacemakers: they shall be recognized as children of God. Inclusive language is wrong here and conceals the meaning of the text. Matthew deliberately chooses the word *huioi* (sons) when he could have used *tekna* (children), which he has used over fifteen times elsewhere. The word "sons" evokes "Son of God" earlier in his Gospel (3:17; 4:3, 6). Also it alludes to its only other occurrence, later in this sermon, when Jesus says: "But I say to you: Love your enemies, and pray for those who persecute you, that you may be sons (*huioi*) of your Father in Heaven."

The peacemakers are those who seek to bring harmony and reconciliation between adversaries. They seek that "tranquillity of order" which St. Augustine defines as the essence of peace. Where there is no opposition or conflict, there is the perfection of peace. But we cannot even attempt to introduce that order into the world unless first we harmonize and reconcile those desires which conflict within ourselves, for as St. James (4:1) explains: "Where do these wars and battles first start? Is it not precisely in the desires fighting in your own selves?" But they are blessed "who, by bringing in order all the motions of their soul, and subjecting them to reason—i.e., to the mind and spirit—and by having their carnal lusts thoroughly subdued, become a kingdom of God."[6] For when the Spirit of God moves over the face of the deep then all is collected. Where Christ reigns in the heart, deep within the souls of the blessed; where all

---

6. St. Augustine, *On the Sermon on the Mount*, 9.

guilt and remorse have been stilled by the reconciliation purchased for us by Our Saviour; and where faith rests, quietly trusting in the Father of all mercies, there is the kingdom of peace.

> In darkness and secure,
> By the secret ladder, disguised,
> —ah, the sheer grace!—
> I went out unseen,
> My house being now all stilled.[7]

Our souls having thus been stilled, "hidden with Christ in God" (Col. 3:3)—subjected to what is from above—we are able to manage with serenity all that is beneath. With poise and equanimity we are able to display to the world a real and substantial peace, well-grounded in the Truth. The prince of this world, having been subdued and cast out, can only storm and thunder outside. Yet his persecutions only serve to strengthen the blessed, who already know their need of God and as a result are moved even more earnestly and deeply to entrust themselves to their Heavenly Father.

Then, just as Christ has reconciled us with the Father, so we are able to participate in the ministry of reconciliation of the peoples with God (2 Cor. 5:19). As such we shall also be recognized "sons of God" which is a title of honour and dignity. St. Thomas commenting on this beatitude said: "The highest place in the palace belongs to the king's son." By allying ourselves with his mission of peace we identify ourselves with the Son of God who is also the Prince of Peace. "Peace I bequeath to you, my own peace I give to you, a peace which the world cannot give, this is my peace to you. Do not let your hearts be troubled or afraid. . . . In the world you will have hardship, but be courageous: I have conquered the world" (Jn. 14: 27; 16:33).

Blessed are those who are persecuted in the cause of uprightness: the kingdom of Heaven is theirs. Blessed are you when people abuse you and persecute you and speak all kinds of calumny against you falsely on my account. Rejoice and be glad, for your reward will be great in

---

7. St. John of the Cross, *Ascent of Mount Carmel.*

Heaven; this is how they persecuted the prophets before you. Our Lord's sudden switch to the word "you" in this last beatitude is masterly. It reveals its entire meaning as well as completing all that has gone before. And because the blessing is the same as that of the first beatitude, thus binding the end to the beginning, the word "you" is singularly consoling. Moreover, it also enables the remainder of the sermon to become more personal.

The key to this beatitude's meaning lies in the words "on my account." It will be instructive for us to consider a few words from John 15:13–20: "No one can have greater love than to lay down his life for his friends. You are my friends, if you do what I command you . . . but because you do not belong to the world, because my choice of you has drawn you out of the world, that is why the world hates you. . . . A servant is not greater than his master. If they persecuted me, they will persecute you" (cf. Mt. 10:17–25). Christians, who are called by Jesus to live a life which goes counter to the dominant culture, will be hated because, as those of that culture themselves admit, it "imposes religion" on them. Such an admission is telling, for by it they confirm that: "This people's heart has grown coarse, their ears dulled, they have shut their eyes tight to avoid using their eyes to see, their ears to hear, their hearts to understand, changing their ways and being healed by me" (Mt. 13:14–15). Precisely because the character of Christ—who manifests all the beatitudes—is reflected in his disciples, these faithful servants stand as accusers, convicting the world of guilt. It is for this reason that the world hates the children of God. It is for this reason that Christians have become the most persecuted religion from North Africa across the Middle East to China and North Korea. It is why they are becoming persecuted in Europe and North America. Nevertheless, if we should endure these persecutions *on account of Jesus*—lay down our lives for him—he considers us friends.

The beatitudes have reached their summit, for the blessed are now identified with the Person of Christ and with his suffering, and so made worthy to receive his merits. In this Our Lord expresses his divine authority. Even so, and for that reason, does he now refer to the blessed as "you." And from now on he will be addressing directly—as "you"—you who are truly standing with him.

4

Surpassing the Law

WE ARE UNITED with God in Christ, knit to him in our faith given to us by the Holy Spirit, through whom and in whom we are heir to all his blessings. From this union surge all our yearnings and aspirations for sanctity for ourselves and for the salvation of others. This is why we, mourn and offer prayers and supplications with deep sighs and groans. Recognizing our wretchedness, we hunger and thirst for righteousness, for purity of heart. We seek, for the world, the same inner peace which perfuses our deeper being and from which, as from a serene and placid spring, upswells our joy. All these virtues combine to perfect his body the Church throughout her members. And from this treasury flow her prayers, merits, and charitable blessings for the salvation of the world.

> 13 You are salt for the earth. But if salt loses its taste, what can make it salty again? It is good for nothing, and can only be thrown out to be trampled under people's feet. 14 You are light for the world. A city built on a hill-top cannot be hidden. 15 No one lights a lamp to put it under a tub; they put it on the lamp-stand where it shines for everyone in the house. 16 In the same way your light must shine in people's sight, so that, seeing your good works, they may give praise to your Father in Heaven.

From the Dead Sea, and from salt mines dug into the elemental earth, came the salt which in ancient Palestine functioned as both a preservative and a purifying agent. Although its use of preservative was widespread, nevertheless it is mainly its use for purification which is emphasized here. After all, the preservative effects of salt arise from its purifying virtues which enable it to destroy putrefying microbes and to expel infestations. The Bible frequently mentions salt as an agent of purification. In Lev. 2:13 we read how salt must be added to the offering in order both to purify it for God and also as a symbol of the covenant. Indeed, "to every offering you will add salt to your God." The incense offered in front of the Testimony before the Tent of Meeting was to be seasoned with "salt, pure and holy" (Ex. 30:35). Even newborn children were either to be cleansed with water or rubbed with salt (Ez. 16:4), because they had been exposed in the open field lying in dirt and blood on the day they were born. Finally, Elijah threw salt into a foul spring in order to purify it; for it had been causing miscarriages among the women of a city which was dependent upon a source of pure water (2 Kgs. 2:21).

The word *moranthe*, often translated as "to lose taste" or "flavour," never had this use in all of ancient literature.[1] A better rendering would be "to become insipid," since the word originally meant to become foolish or feeble-minded (*moros*). For those disciples have indeed become foolish who having "tasted the goodness of God's message and the powers of the world to come –and yet in spite of this have fallen away—it is impossible for them to be brought to the freshness of repentance a second time" (Heb. 6:5–6). For just as salt which has lost its savor is "good for nothing, and can only be thrown out to be trampled under people's feet," so it also falls to those who, having first received the good news of the kingdom, then deliberately become hardened or indifferent to its animating Spirit. They will find themselves trampled underfoot by the world: choked by its teachings, distracted by its allures. They are like the seed sown among the thorns where "the worry of the world and lure of riches choke the word and so it produces nothing" (Mt. 13:22). Or, perhaps, they are among those who, through lack of depth of understanding, fear the persecutions and calumnies of this world. "Should some trial come, or some persecution on account of the word, at once he falls away" (13:21). It is foolish to stoop to clasp the things that are beneath only to be trodden under the feet of worldly traffic. Much more salutary it is to savor those things from above. "Have salt in yourselves and be at peace with one another!" (Mk. 9:50).

---

1. Charles Quarles, *The Sermon on the Mount* (Nashville: B&H Publishing Group, 2011), p. 81.

Similarly, you are also the light of the world. And just as the disciple who has been salted with the word of God, cannot help but represent purity to a corrupted world, so the soul that has been illuminated by the good news of the kingdom of God, must allow her light to shine through her good works. Such a purified person must not hide one's light from fear of persecution or derision. Nor must one conceal it for reasons of scrupulosity or from false humility. Rather the proper motive must be "to give glory to your Father who is in Heaven."

Jesus uses the metaphor of a city upon a hill. The word translated hill (*orous*) is the same word for the mountain upon which Our Lord was seated at the time. "Mountain" would, therefore, immediately conjure up among his listeners the image of Mount Zion which Isaiah has prophesied will, in the final days: "rise higher than the mountains and tower above the heights." All the nations will stream to it saying: "Come, let us go up to the mountain of YHWH, to the house of the God of Jacob that he may teach us his ways so that we may walk in his paths. . . . House of Jacob come, let us walk in YHWH's light" (2:2–3, 5).

Isaiah identifies the speaker of the message as his suffering servant: "Here is my servant whom I uphold, my chosen one in whom my soul delights. . . . I have made you a covenant of the people and light to the nations. . . ." (42:6). This passage from Isaiah is applied by Matthew, himself, to Jesus (12:18–21). Again in the second song of the servant (49:6) we find: "I shall make you a light to the nations so that my salvation may reach to the remotest parts of the earth." This is the same servant who in Isaiah 50 and 53 would endure blows and insults, be despised and rejected, but who would "justify many by taking their guilt upon himself" (53:11).

These are powerful allusions which we, following the author of the *Epistle to Diognetus*,[2] may also apply to those servants whom the Lord considers his friends: those who do what he commands and who suffer for his sake.

---

2. Ch. 5. This document was discovered in 1435 in a fish market in Constantinople by an Italian student, Thomas of Arezzo. Its anonymous author claims: "Although I am an instructor of the Gentiles now, I was once a disciple (*mathetes*)

Though destiny has placed them here in the flesh, they do not live after the flesh; their days are passed on earth, but their citizenship is above in the Heavens. They obey the prescribed laws, but in their own private lives they transcend the laws. They show love to all men—and all men persecute them. They are misunderstood, and condemned; yet by suffering death they are quickened into life. They are poor, yet making many rich; lacking all things, yet having all things in abundance. They are dishonoured, yet made glorious in their very dishonour; slandered, yet vindicated.

This is the dignity of the *anawim*—the people of God—you who are devoted to the Lord, who belong to his kingdom and are heir to his blessings. By faith you are united to Jesus Christ who, through his Holy Spirit, lives and reigns within you, illuminating your souls. All your blessings and virtues flow from God's Truth into you, his image, now joined to him in that kingdom of Heaven enthroned within your hearts.

You who constitute this new people of God comprise his visible kingdom on earth. For this reason it follows that you are the salt of the earth, and light for the world. Therefore, you who contemplate the light within, should not hide that light; for just as the eye is a lamp to the body (Mt. 6:22) so you are the light of the world. The difficulty is to actualize this: to walk in that Spirit and by him sanctify all you encounter.

¹⁷ Do not imagine that I have come to abolish the Law or the Prophets. I have come not to abolish but to complete them. ¹⁸ In truth I tell you, till Heaven and earth disappear, not one dot, not one little stroke, is to disappear from the Law until all its purpose is achieved. ¹⁹ Therefore, anyone who infringes even one of the least of these commandments and teaches others to do the same will be considered the least in the kingdom of Heaven; but the person who keeps them and teaches them will be considered great in the kingdom of Heaven. ²⁰ For I tell you, if your uprightness does

---

of the Apostles; and what was then delivered to me, I now minister faithfully to students of the truth."(11) This "epistle" also situates itself during a time when the Jews were still "fulfilling their sacrificial duty to [God] by means of blood and the smoke of sacrifices and burnt-offerings."(3) Its exact date is disputed.

not surpass that of the scribes and Pharisees, you will never get into the kingdom of Heaven.

Lest the people of God should presume that their status in the kingdom exempts them from fulfilling the precepts of the tradition, or that perhaps Jesus' new kingdom somehow supplants the law, Our Lord, knowing human hypocrisy, hastens to stress that not one minutiae of the law is to disappear until it has fulfilled its purpose. Haggadah cannot exist without halakhah: the Spirit cannot exist without the Word.

This passage coheres well with the previous message about salt and light. Our actions must convict the world about law and about truth. This witness will, like leaven, set in motion all that the Lord intends for the world and for the enduring people of God. For the law must continue to fulfil its purpose of: testing virtue, sanctifying the saints, convicting the world of sin, separating sheep from goats, manifesting and corroborating the justice of the Last Judgement, and confirming the merits of the just.

> The heart is more deceitful than any other thing,
>   and exceedingly corrupt—who can understand it?
> I YHWH search the mind and try the heart,
>   to give each person according to his ways,
>   according to the merit of his deeds.[3]

In the end all hypocrisy, lies, and evil shall be exposed, and the righteousness of the saints will be vindicated. Though the heavens and the earth may disappear, nothing of the law will pass away until all this is accomplished. Our Lord is unveiling for us the mystery of the kingdom of Heaven.

In order for all this to be fulfilled it is mandatory that the blessed do not infringe even the least of the commandments. Neither must they teach others to do so. Our righteousness must exceed that of those who do relax or distort the commandments, those who are identified by Jesus as the scribes and the Pharisees. So who then were the scribes and the Pharisees?

In the first century, the scribes and the Pharisees formed two

---

3. Jer. 17:9–10.

distinct sections in Jewish society; although it was possible for some scribes also to belong to the Pharisaic party. The scribes were the professional interpreters of the law in the synagogues of every village and town. They could draft legal contracts for marriage, divorce, loans, inheritance, mortgages, real estate, etc. Their origin dates from the return from the Babylonian Captivity. The earliest mention of the title occurs in Ezra 7:6, 10 where Ezra is described as a "ready scribe in the law of Moses. . . . For Ezra had devoted himself to studying the law of YHWH so as to put into practice and teach its statutes and rulings." The law was revered as the precise expression of the will of God binding on every pious Jew whose life was regulated to the minutest detail. They were held in high esteem often seen wearing distinctive robes and occupying prominent places in the synagogue.

The Pharisees, in contrast, were members of a faction in Judaism who formed at various times a political party, a social movement, and a school of thought. The name *Pharisee* means *the separated ones*. They were also known as *chasidim,* which means *loyal to God,* or *loved of God.* They rose to power under the Hasmonean dynasty (140–37 BC) in the aftermath of the Maccabean Revolt against Antiochus IV (Epiphanes). Pharisees were members of a party that believed in tithing, ritual cleansing, and strict Sabbath observance. Unlike the aristocratic and scripturally conservative Sadducees who only acknowledged the five books of Moses, the Pharisees believed in the resurrection and followed legal traditions that were ascribed, not only to the Torah, but also to the halakhic and haggadic traditions of the fathers (which had been codified into the Mishnah and later the Gemarah). Like the scribes, they were also well-known legal experts. But unlike the scribes, the Pharisees were small landowners and traders—not a professional establishment. After the destruction of the Second Temple in AD 70, Pharisaic beliefs became the liturgical and didactic basis for the office of Rabbi within later Judaism.

Thus, when Jesus demanded a righteousness that exceeded the scribes and the Pharisees, he was not referring so much to their adherence to the law as such, for he had already said that he himself did not intend for the law to be abolished. Rather, as is made clear in all four Gospels,[4] it was to their hypocrisy—i.e., their tendency to interpret the law in such a way as to moderate or even to nullify its demands—to which he directed his rebukes. An example of this tendency is given in Matthew 15:3–6:

> And why do you break away from the commandment of God for the sake of your tradition? For God said "Honour your father and your mother" and "Anyone who curses his father or mother will be put to death." But you say, "If anyone says to his father or mother: 'Anything I might have used to help you is dedicated to God,' he is rid of his duty to father or mother." In this way you have made God's word ineffective by means of your tradition.

The real danger was that the scribes and the Pharisees were not only refusing to enter the kingdom of Heaven themselves, but were also effectively keeping the people, *for whom they were responsible*, from their inheritance of the covenanted kingdom. This is clear from Jesus' diatribe to the Pharisees: "you shut the kingdom of Heaven against men; for you neither enter yourselves, nor allow those who would enter to go in" (Mt. 23:13; Mk. 9:42 = Lk. 17:1–2). The charge is deadly serious, for the Son of God was obviously just and apt to reprove their hypocrisy, blindness, and self-serving righteousness. He declared that they were making others "twice as much a child of hell" as themselves (Mt. 23:15). This, of course, is the real point at issue: their religion was only an external one, bereft of any genuine life in the Spirit. Yet their perceived authority was leading many astray.

In order to be great in the kingdom of Heaven it is essential that one's example and teaching is in conformity with the commandments. Do the truly devout aspire to anything less? Simple piety and authenticity of discipleship demand this. We are called to be holy as Our Heavenly Father is holy. And, since this is to be reflected in all we say and do, it follows that we shall be fulfilling this injunction providing we also avoid hypocrisy: the hypocrisy of the scribes and Pharisees that Jesus so deplored.

However, to infringe even the least of the commandments, and to

4. Mt. 23:1–36; Mk. 12:37–40; Lk. 11:37–53; Jn. 5:39–37.

teach others by one's words and actions to do the same is to be considered least in the kingdom. Although we may not have committed or encouraged others to commit a grave sin, nevertheless, we may have shown a negligence and contempt towards venial sins that could even jeopardize our own and others entry into the kingdom of Heaven. For unless our righteousness exceeds the scribes and the Pharisees we shall in no wise enter that kingdom.

Jesus, therefore, does not need to say here what will happen to those who encourage others to disobey the *greater* of the commandments, since his statement regarding what happens to those who teach others to break the *least* commandment is meant as an understatement. By having ranked them beneath the least in the kingdom, how much worse it would be for those who enticed others to graver matters! Jesus is using a customary rabbinic form of rhetorical argument (*litotes*) here.

> [21]You have heard how it was said to our ancestors, You shall not kill; and if anyone does kill he must answer for it before the court. [22]But I say this to you, anyone who is angry with a brother will answer for it before the court; anyone who calls a brother "Fool" will answer for it before the Sanhedrin; and anyone who calls him "Traitor" will answer for it in hell fire. [23]So then, if you are bringing your offering to the altar and there remember that your brother has something against you, [24]leave your offering there before the altar, go and be reconciled with your brother first, and then come back and present your offering. [25]Come to terms with your opponent in good time while you are still on the way to the court with him, or he may hand you over to the judge and the judge to the officer, and you will be thrown into prison. [26]In truth I tell you, you will not get out till you have paid the last penny.

Here begin a set of utterances labelled "the antitheses" because they start with the disjunction "you have heard ... but I say." In these antitheses we find combined our first and second principles, where Jesus asserts his authority over those who would dispute with him. Having raised the issue of external religion among the biblical scholars and clerics of his day, Jesus now gives several examples of the differences in application of external versus internal religion. Our Lord is illustrating how our righteousness must exceed that of the scribes and the Pharisees. We are being called to heroic virtue.

Yet the real menace to internal religion comes not merely from a few errant scholars or a clutch of addled clerics. The more imminent danger emerges from the "Pharisees" within—from our own tendencies to self-deception and self-righteousness. "If then the light inside you is darkness, how great is that darkness!" (Mt. 6:23). We may speak truly to others when we can look in the mirror and ask ourselves: "Do I really know this? Is my claim to Truth so assured that I would stake eternal life on it?" Then I can wipe the night from my eyes and let in the light of the morning.

Thus Our Lord begins with the matter of killing; for there are many ways to extinguish the light. Jesus quotes the fifth commandment given in Ex. 20:13 and Dt. 5:17, "You shall not murder." The word "murder" is a better translation than "kill" since both the Bible and the tradition of the Church allow for killing in self-defence, in a just war, or killing animals for food. But by murder is meant the taking of an innocent life as occurs in homicide, abortion, euthanasia, or even in reducing a person to ruin.

Such acts are a violation of divine law: hence the statement that one "must answer for it before the court." The Greek word *krisis* can mean either judgement, tribunal, or court. A literal interpretation in favour of any one of these terms misses the haggadic form of Christ's teaching. Throughout this passage there is an affinity of meaning between "judgement," "court," "Sanhedrin," and "altar." Having already heard him refer to "our ancestors," i.e., those who received the law given to Moses by God, it should be apparent that Jesus is not making any distinction between secular and divine judgement. The secular law in this case is also the divine law. Therefore, Our Lord's meaning is that any such criminal action renders us accused before God as well. The ultimate authority behind the law is one in either case.

But there is another form of murder, and that is to assassinate another person's reputation: to ruin an individual's life. Slander is also a sin against the fifth commandment. And it rises from the same disordered emotions as does physical murder. Thus, even to express violent anger (the Greek word *orge* means to fume with rage) towards someone is to have already destroyed a profound mutuality between oneself and that person, namely that we are all children of God, made in his image and likeness. This gives us a ponderous dignity upon which our duty to others fundamentally rests; since we cannot deny to others the very dignity that is also ours. This dignity is the foundation of their rights as well—indeed, of all rights. Therefore, to attack that image in another is to nullify it in ourselves. But even worse, it is to alienate us from one another and thereby undo what ultimately binds us to our neighbour: namely, that we all share the same ontic nature analogous to the divine Being, our Exemplar. Even to lie to another is to judge derisively: it is to say "you are not worthy of the truth." Such a condemnation is not ours to make.

Even more reprehensible is to call someone a fool (Gk. *raka*). Yet to persist in this and then go on to call someone an idiot or moron (Gk. *moros*) betrays a deliberate and enduring anathema to another individual. Most commentators dwell upon the comparative degrees of severity between these terms attempting to justify the relative consequences pursuant to each act. But there is really very little difference between the terms "fool" and "moron." Instead what Jesus is asserting is that the accuser has persisted in this contumely without making any attempt towards forgiveness or reconciliation. Repeating something three times was a traditional means of emphasis. Thus to continue in this rancor, not only twice but three times, *a fortiori* reinforces the culpability of the aggressor so that the repercussions upon one, and upon the state of one's soul, gradually worsen. Jesus is saying that enduring *unrepentant* anger towards another individual shall render the aggressor liable (*enokos*) to the hell of fire (*gehenna tou pyros*).

It follows from the above interpretation that our duty towards our wronged brethren is to seek reconciliation before we can single-heartedly make a devout offering at the altar before God. Our Lord is only repeating an injunction made previously in the Torah which taught that before a worshipper offered a sacrifice for a sin against someone else one must first make payment to the one who is wronged (Num. 5:5–8). In other words it is not just a matter of personal hypocrisy, but it is a matter of the state of one's soul. Before one can make an acceptable offering one must be in a state of grace. Therefore, if we remember any sin against our brother we must first be reconciled with him. This action is so mandatory that we must actually leave the altar to seek him out—even if it meant for Jesus' listeners to travel from the altar of sacrifice in Jerusalem back to Galilee (some 200 km)! Only then may we return to offer our gifts to God with clean hearts.

That is also the meaning of the extended metonymy which follows. Being brought before the court represents being brought before the council of God. As we have seen above, the secular law in Israel was regarded as being one with the divine law. The courts were acting vicariously in carrying out the sentence of that law. To avoid being sentenced you must "come to terms with your accuser quickly" ... "on the way." Origen, Ss. Cyprian, Hilary, Ambrose, Jerome, Augustine, Bede and Gregory all variously affirm that "on the way" symbolizes the passage of this present life, that the "accuser" is our conscience (the worm that will never die), that the judge stands for the Lord, that the prison is a figure for purgatory, and that the "last penny" represents the least venial sin which must be atoned for.[5]

There can be no genuine rest for those poor souls who sincerely love the Lord until they can make up to him for all the wrong they have done him. It would distress them to desire less. Love does not take the beloved for granted. How crass and selfish it would be, for example, for a husband who has wronged his wife and is sincerely sorry, to neglect to try to make up to her for the wrong he has done. His love and honour for her would prevent him from such a disrespectful and uncaring rebuff. How could he ever honestly look her in the eyes again? And even less so if the Beloved is Our Blessed Lord!

Yet we are the bride of Christ.[6] Therefore, so much more is this the condition for those who deeply and genuinely love the Lord. It is only natural and just for the human soul to want to make reparation to the One we have offended, particularly for those offences we

---

5. Dave Armstrong, *A Biblical Defence of Catholicism* (Manchester: Sophia Institute, 2003), p.129.

6. Mt. 25:1; Mk. 2:19; Jn. 3:29; 2 Cor. 11:2–4; Eph. 5:22–33; Rev. 19:7; 22:17.

have committed after we have been regenerated or reborn through grace. Of course Christ forgives us. But it does not make it any the less distressing to have to look into the eyes of the Lord, only to see mercy, compassion, and forgiveness gazing back, while realizing that it is expressly against such charity that the soul has offended. Moreover, God's love for the poor souls is such that he, himself, desires that they be established in all uprightness. He could never leave them in the state of everlasting remorse. But purgatory affords one the opportunity to say: "My God, I am sorry for having offended Thee who are so good." Being thus reconciled, with all their sins purged and forgotten, their tears having been wiped from their eyes, they are at peace. They may at last look lovingly upon the eyes of their Saviour. "Blessed are the peacemakers for they shall be called sons of God."

> [27] You have heard how it was said, You shall not commit adultery. [28] But I say this to you, if a man looks at a woman lustfully, he has already committed adultery with her in his heart. [29] If your right eye should be your downfall, tear it out and throw it away; for it will do you less harm to lose one part of yourself than to have your whole body thrown into hell. [30] And if your right hand should be your downfall, cut it off and throw it away; for it will do you less harm to lose one part of yourself than to have your whole body go to hell.

Jesus now moves from the fifth to the sixth commandment. Once again he is illustrating how our righteousness must exceed that of the scribes and the Pharisees in order for it to be a genuine religion of the heart. Thus, while one must certainly not commit adultery (Dt. 5:18), Jesus requires that whoever even looks on a woman to lust after her (*lit.* looking at a woman in order to desire her) has already committed adultery with her in his heart. Here Jesus has conjoined the sixth commandment with the ninth: "You shall not covet your neighbour's wife" (Dt. 5:21). Similar prohibitions are to be found elsewhere in the Old Testament (Job 31:1, 9–12; Sirach 9:5). In fact, Christ's prohibition does not exceed that of a number of rabbis who also warned of the same thing. For example, it was rabbinic teaching that, "He who commits adultery with his eyes is also called an adulterer."[7] Clearly this does not exempt women from the same prohibition. In those days Jewish women were required to be modest and were admonished not to venture out of the house alone unless in the company of other women. Also they practised custody of the eyes and veiled their faces when in the presence of men (Gen. 24:65, 38:14). In any case, in the predominantly masculine culture of Jewish Palestine, the lustful look was considered to be a weakness mainly characteristic of men.

What matters here is the intention of looking at a woman *in order* to desire her. It is the deliberate continued salacious leer that is blameworthy. This is wrong not simply because it objectifies the woman. Although, that is bad enough since it denies her the dignity of her personhood: i.e., it profanes the image of God in her. What is really censurable—even if the woman is unaware of this look—is the offence such a lewd disposition in the man presents to God. Once again the ontological order of things is disrupted and the man has perverted something that God had created for good. As it was with anger or slander, the fabric of the divine economy has been torn. Disorder has intruded into creation . . . from within. "For from the heart come evil intentions: murder, adultery, fornication, theft, perjury, slander" (Mt. 15:19).

Thus, when we consider the betrayal to God, which such a revolt against the divine economy involves, it is not surprising then that the prophets should continuously regard the sins of Israel as adultery. In Isaiah (57:3) YHWH calls the nation an "adulterous race." Hosea's wife Gomer, the adulteress, was for him a figure of all the sins of Israel. His entire book plays on this theme. Jeremiah depicts Judah as having "committed adultery with stones and pieces of wood" (3:9; see also 5:7; 7:9; 23:14). Ezekiel, in an allegorical history of the sins of Jerusalem and Samaria, likewise presents their idolatries as a litany of adulteries (cp. 23). He likens Jerusalem to an adulterous wife who "welcomes strangers instead of her husband" (16:32) and compares her sins to those of Sodom and Samaria (v. 46). Even so he considers those of Jerusalem to be "more revolting than theirs, they are more upright than you are" (v.52).

7. Charles Quarles, *Sermon on the Mount*, p. 116, nn. 92 and 93.

The God of the covenant is the spouse of Israel. The prophets were able to allegorize this pledge as a marriage because, in the natural union between a man and a woman and in the covenantal relationship of YHWH with Israel, both are grounded upon a fecunditive communion between the "husband" and the "bride." Just as God blessed Adam and Eve commanding them to "be fruitful, multiply, fill the earth and subdue it" so Christ could say regarding the new Israel: "I will tell you, then, that the kingdom of God will be taken from you and given to a people who will produce its fruit" (Mt. 21:43).

Herein lies the mystery of the interconnection between creation and free will. Physical science and modal logic together affirm that underlying the structure of all matter is a surging sea of virtual futures. So that when a free action is performed, these probability waves, as it were, collapse; and we pick out of all possible worlds the one remaining alternative which the cosmos will actually realize. Our actions give form to the passive potentials of primal matter, weaving into the very fabric of space-time the consequences of our implementation of freewill: the cosmos is meant for moral stewardship. Then the good that we should have done is left undone forever; and the evil we could have avoided is now loosed to stream down the ages. God's economy is ruptured: the temporal order has been altered for all time. "The whole of creation is groaning in travail." Therefore, God's eternal justice demands that this breach must be repaired.

This modern age denies the seriousness of sin. Or else it is simply deemed a personal matter only and, therefore, could not possibly merit the ultimate penalty that the Son of God decrees. Nevertheless, this does not negate the fact that sin is a deliberate betrayal of a covenant with the Lord; that it upsets the just order he requires; that it spreads harmful ripples throughout the populace; and that it all flows from our own free will. Thus Our Lord's hyperbole—to pluck out the guilty eye or to cut off the offending hand—does not strike us as strained. The heart must be purified by cutting off sin before it coalesces in the will. For God justly reserves Heaven only for those who show themselves willing to be purified of all that is unholy in their hearts. The free and wilful refusal to do so, by obstinately clinging to immorality, is but to constitute one's soul fit for eternal reprobation. "Blessed are the pure in heart for they shall see God."

> [31]It has also been said, Anyone who divorces his wife must give her a writ of dismissal. [32]But I say this to you, everyone who divorces his wife, except for the case of an illicit marriage, makes her an adulteress; and anyone who marries a divorced woman commits adultery.

Having dealt with the nature of adultery, Jesus now moves on to deal with the indissolubility of marriage. We have seen that marriage was regarded throughout the Old Testament as a covenant which prefigured that between God and his people. In emphasizing the indissolubility of marriage, except in the case of adultery, Jesus goes back, beyond rabbinic opinions to the original intention of the law. Most of the opinions found among some commentators on this issue have arisen from their various theories of scripture. Noting that only Matthew has the "exception" clause (see Lk. 16:18; Mk. 10:11–12), they are at pains to explain its origin. So they argue, depending on how they order these Gospels, that some hypothetical redactor had either added or deleted the phrase in question. But to use an unprovable theory to substantiate one's conclusions is to make an unwarranted claim to truth. Nevertheless, it is Matthew's account that forms the basis for Church teaching on this issue, and it will inform our present discussion.[8]

We begin with a quotation which sums up both Our Lord's and the Church's teaching:

> And here is something else you do: you cover the altar of YHWH with tears, with weeping and wailing, because he now refuses to consider the offering or to accept it from you. And you ask, "Why?" Because YHWH stands as witness between you and the wife of your youth, with whom you have broken faith, even though she was your partner and your wife by covenant. Did he not create a single being, having flesh and the breath of life? And what does this single being seek? God-given offspring! Have

---

8. See *CCC* 2380–2385 and *The Code of Canon Law* 1152.

respect for your own life then, and do not break faith with the wife of your youth. For I hate divorce, says YHWH, God of Israel, and people concealing their cruelty under a cloak, says YHWH Sabaoth. Have respect for your own life then, and do not break faith. (Mal. 13–16)

Our Lord's meaning will be made even clearer if we also take into consideration Christ's teaching in Matthew 19:3–5: "Have you not read that the Creator from the beginning made them male and female and that he said: 'This is why a man leaves his father and mother and becomes attached to his wife, and the two become one flesh.' They are no longer two, therefore, but one flesh. So then, what God has united, let no one separate." By the phrase "from the beginning" Jesus is referring to the creation (See Gen. 1:27–28; 2:24). Our Lord is declaring that from the beginning a licit marriage was between *one* man and *one* woman only, the implication being that death alone is able to separate them. (See Ro. 7:2; 1 Cor. 7:39.) Marriage, then, is for life because it is a covenant between the two male and female parties and their Creator. Therefore, such a promise made before God (*coram Deo*) cannot be as lightly dismissed as some of the rabbis of Jesus' time contended.

The exception which Jesus gives, "except in the case of adultery (*porneia*)," permits separation only "if that spouse has not either expressly or tacitly condoned the other's fault, he or she [sic] has the right to sever the common conjugal life, provided he or she [sic] has not consented to the adultery, nor been the cause of it, nor also committed adultery" (Can. 1152.1). The Greek word *porneia* is the basis for the transliterated word fornication. (The only difference is that the unvoiced labial plosive "p" has been replaced by the unvoiced labial fricative "f" which often occurs in borrowed words.) Fornication refers to any sexual act outside the matrimonial unit, i.e., any illicit sexual act. Only the union between a man and a woman is licit under divine law. Fornication is always wrong whether at least one person is married, but not to the other party, (in which case it constitutes adultery *in ipso*); or neither of them is married. (See Mt. 15:9; Acts 15:20; Ro. 1:29; 1 Cor. 5:1; 6:9, 13, 18; Jude 7; all of which use the word *porneia*.) Adultery is a form of *porneia* because, like the idolatries of Israel, it is the betrayal of the sacredness of the divine covenant. This covenant forms the authoritative basis for all the other covenants among the people of God, and should not be undone.

Actually, a careful reading of Dt. 24:1–4 does not give it the force the rabbis needed to argue for a writ of divorce. Moses was actually exemplifying one type of complication that could arise, *viz.*, that the man's act of issuing a writ of divorce actually makes his wife unclean should she marry again; and neither can he take her back. Jesus is saying much the same thing; for he also goes on to say that anyone marrying her will also commit adultery. The implication of Our Lord's teaching is codified in Can. 1152.1: "It is earnestly recommended that a spouse, motivated by Christian charity and solicitous for the good of the family, should not refuse to pardon an adulterous partner and should not sunder the conjugal life." Reading carefully the text of the sermon one will see that this is Our Lord's teaching as well. It is almost a condensation of the teaching of Moses, but in such a manner as to bring out the deeper principle involved. Marriage is an indissoluble union and to put away one's wife, *even if she were innocent*, exposes her to the prospect of adultery also. This also explains the closing phrase "and anyone who marries a divorced woman commits adultery." Once again we can see the series of harmful effects that can ensue upon breaking a divine law. Disrupt God's order, and disaster of necessity follows.

In a few well-chosen words, Our Blessed Saviour has discouraged divorce, refuted the misinterpretations of the rabbis, uncovered the true meaning of the law, censured fornication, protected the innocent, and upheld the sanctity and inviolability of marriage *coram Deo*. Moreover, by showing concern for the innocent, he has uncovered the truth that marriage is based on love, and that love includes forgiveness.

Hosea 11:1–2, 8–9 gives us a touching expression of the profound love that YHWH has for his people, Israel:

> When Israel was a child, I loved him,
> And out of Egypt I called my son
> The more I called them,

the more they went from me;
they kept sacrificing to the Baals,
and burning incense to idols.

. . .

How can I give you up, O Ephraim!
How can I hand you over, O Israel!
My heart recoils within me,
My compassion grows warm and tender.
I will not execute my fierce anger,
I will not again destroy Ephraim;
for I am God and not man,
the Holy One in your midst,
and I will not come to destroy.

After having received the warnings of so many prophets with indifference and even hostility, and after having suffered the ensuing dénouement of destruction and exile, Israel finally grasped the reality of her flagrant adulteries. She desired to be freed from her captivity. Convicted of her betrayal, Israel grieved for that kingdom of righteousness originally promised by YHWH to the People of the Covenant. Her contrition disclosed her renewal of heart. In the end, moved by her abundant penances and her sorrowful petitions, the Lord forgave errant Israel and, lifting her from exile, restored her to her house. "Blessed are those who hunger and thirst for righteousness: for they shall be filled."

[33] Again, you have heard how it was said to our ancestors, You must not break your oath, but must fulfil your oaths to the Lord. [34] But I say this to you, do not swear at all, either by Heaven, since that is God's throne; [35] or by earth, since that is his footstool; or by Jerusalem, since that is the city of the great King. [36] Do not swear by your own head either, since you cannot turn a single hair white or black. [37] All you need say is "Yes" if you mean yes, "No" if you mean no; anything more than this comes from the Evil One.

The New Covenant which we, the people of God, have in Christ Jesus has secured us in a unique relationship with Our Heavenly Father. This has been actuated through our faith in the Son, and is written on our hearts, so that we may live out our lives from this new being within. With regard to each of the three commandments exemplified above, Our Lord has explained how his devoted disciples must live beyond mere adherence to the letter of the law and attain to its true meaning. In each case a profound authenticity was required from each of us as is befitting of the Blessed. Having dealt with three examples from the Ten Commandments, Our Lord now elucidates what our deeper life involves with three more examples taken from the rabbinic law.

The phrase, "You must not break your oath, but must fulfil your oaths to the Lord," is not a direct quotation from the Old Testament, but rather a rabbinic paraphrase of several verses such as: Num. 30:3 and Dt. 23:22–24; or Ps. 50:14. This rabbinic interpretation was designed to affirm that only oaths made to the Lord, to the divine name, must be strictly adhered to; while those oaths made on the basis of some other authority do not have to carry such a solemn weight. Hence statements such as "by Heaven," "by the land (of Israel)," "by Jerusalem," or even "on my own head be it," were each considered by degrees to be less binding than any oath made to God. Once again the underlying intention is to somehow circumvent the need to keep one's oath.

> Alas for you, blind guides! You say, "If anyone swears by the Temple, it has no force but anyone who swears by the gold of the Temple is bound." Fools and blind! For which is of greater value, the gold or the Temple that makes the gold sacred? Again "If anyone swears by the altar it has no force; but anyone who swears by the offering on the altar, is bound." You blind men! For which is of greater worth, the offering or the altar that makes the offering sacred? Therefore, someone who swears by the altar is swearing by that and by everything on it. And someone who swears by the Temple is swearing by that and by the One who dwells in it. And someone who swears by Heaven is swearing by the throne of God and by the One who is seated there. (Mt. 23:16–22)

To swear in this manner by anything betrays one's hypocrisy, because all things belong to God equally and, therefore, are not ours to use for deceptive means. Heaven is God's throne and is not ours to swear by: we have no right to such proprietorship. It is equally the same to the earth which is God's footstool, or to Jerusalem which belongs to the Davidic King, or even to our own heads, because we have no power to change its condition. This false usurpation of sovereignty especially with the intention of relaxing the relative strength of our oaths is deceptive and disingenuous.

It is preferable not to swear at all by any of these things if the implication is that, because we cannot normally be believed, so in this exceptional case we must take an oath. It is as if someone were to say: "Well, to be honest…" with the implication that one is not ordinarily so. The moment one says, as it were, "cross my heart" then that person has forever condemned oneself as normally untrustworthy. Rather, if we are known to be people of our word, then it is not necessary to swear at all, for we are always to be trustworthy. Say "yes" if you mean yes, and "no" if you mean no. Any other attempt to justify oneself implies the very opposite from what one intends in the first place. Such duplicity comes "from evil."

None of this precludes us from obeying "Caesar" when he requires us to swear in a court of law. Such formality does not contradict Our Lord's teaching that we must be a people of integrity in our normal dealings with others. However, in a world as dishonest and fraudulent as this one is, if the secular authorities require a solemn oath from us, then, since this does not involve any deceit on our parts, there is no difficulty. It is only the duplicity and potential hypocrisy inherent in the manner of oath taking of the scribes and Pharisees to which Our Lord is objecting. Our Lord's real meaning is given in Lev. 19:11–13: "You will not … deal deceitfully or fraudulently with one another. You will not swear by my name with intent to deceive and thus profane the name of your God. I am YHWH." (See also Zech. 8:16–17.)

The honesty and integrity that Christ Jesus requires are nothing more than a genuine poverty of spirit: a spirit in which there is no guile, no ulterior motive springing from false attachments to worldly things. For what do we have which is not from God? Neither Heaven, nor earth, nor the temple, nor our own physical condition is fundamentally ours. Once we admit that all things belong to God after all, and that we are dependent upon him for all that we receive, then it becomes scandalous to imagine that we somehow have some absolute proprietorship over the things that fall under our stewardship. Thus we need not fear lest we might lose some control or dominance that in reality we never have possessed; and as a result strive to manipulate things and people to our own advantage. All things, including time, belong to God ultimately, we being but the stewards of his kingdom. Even our bodies are not our own, but must be used for the glory of God (1 Cor. 6:19–20). This is the essence of detachment, the secret of holiness, and the life of the true contemplative, who, in complete self-abandonment lives only from God and for God (1 Cor. 10:31). Then there can be no duplicity, since in truth we have nothing, and can do nothing of ourselves.

But in Christ we can do all things. The kingdom of Heaven is nothing more than the reign of Christ in our hearts. This is a reality which is being actualized in us through his Spirit, if only we do not frustrate it. It can only be received through spiritual poverty: through emptying oneself of all that impedes or separates us from God. "Now the end of the commandment is charity issuing from a clean heart, a good conscience, and an unfeigned faith" (1 Tim. 1:5). Superficiality and arrogance have no place in the kingdom of Heaven. The tendency not to mean what we say, but instead to equivocate and contrive when dealing with others, comes from a fundamental refusal to situate ourselves squarely in the truth. The reality for us, the people of God, is that the Lord is our centre and not our false ego, which is merely an artificial social and psychological construction—a product of our conditioning which is a consequence of our having internalized the dominant culture. We must challenge this conditioning by constantly asking "is this true, is this culture telling me the truth?" But you, the blessed in the Lord, have the Word of eternal life. Unfeigned faith cannot doubt this. It follows that life in the kingdom comes from denying ourselves and living from this centre which is Christ the Word. To order all things to him is simply spiritual integrity and intellectual honesty: it is truly to express ourselves in divine worship rather than self-worship. And this cannot come about until we acknowledge our spiritual poverty: the fact of our utter dependence on God for all things. "Blessed are the poor in spirit for theirs is the kingdom of Heaven."

38 You have heard how it was said: Eye for eye and tooth for tooth.
39 But I say this to you: offer no resistance to the wicked. On the

contrary, if anyone hits you on the right cheek, offer him the other as well; ⁴⁰if someone wishes to go to law with you to get your tunic, let him have your cloak as well. ⁴¹And if anyone requires you to go one mile, go two miles with him. ⁴²Give to anyone who asks you, and if anyone wants to borrow, do not turn away.

Authentic religion of the heart begins with devotion. Genuine devotion leads to obedience which is the essence of meekness. Having asserted regarding oaths that we must always express the truth, it is natural for the incarnate Wisdom to turn to the question of justice: for there is more to justice than simple retaliation.

The scribes and the Pharisees had interpreted the *lex talionis* in a manner which made charity almost impossible. Exodus 21:24–25 reads: "you will award life for life, eye for eye, tooth for tooth, hand for hand, foot for foot, burn for burn, wound for wound, stroke for stroke." Although this law of retaliation was intended to prevent undue harshness or unjust recompense when setting the punishment for a crime, nevertheless the tendency of the rabbis was to exploit this precept for exacting personal requital. Rabbi Eliezer ben Hyrcanus in the first century maintained that "eye for eye" meant exactly what it said, as did Philo.[9] Even so, Leviticus 19:18 forbids personal vengeance: "You shall not take vengeance, nor bear any grudge against the children of your people; you shall love your neighbour as yourself; I am YHWH." (See also Pr. 24:29). Clearly the *lex talionis* was not intended as a pretext for revenge.

Our Lord did not retaliate when he was slapped upon the cheek. Neither did he even complain when he yielded his torso to the lash; nor when he offered up his face to be spat upon, his cheek to be struck, or his scalp to be punctured by a crown of spines. Without a word he let himself be dragged now to Caiaphas, now to Pilate, then to Herod, and back to Pilate again. The divine Judge of the world willingly submitted to the perfidy of an illegal religious court and to the pretentiousness of imperial adjudication. And though he was pressed to walk to his death, Our Saviour did so bearing an abrasive and heavy cross. Stripped naked of his garments, the Son of God left them to be divided among the four soldiers, and relinquished his

---

9. Charles Quarles, *The Sermon on the Mount*, p.146.

seamless robe as a gambler's trophy. He opened his hands to receive the nails, surrendered his feet to be pegged immobilized to a tree, and bared his bosom to the spear's thrust. And his response to all this was: "Forgive them for they know not what they do."

Was he a doormat then? In these instants we must say he was! "I gave my back to the smiters, and my cheeks to those who pulled out the beard; I hid not my face from shame and spitting." . . . "He was oppressed, and he was afflicted, yet he opened not his mouth; like a lamb that is led to the slaughter, and like a sheep that is before its shearers is dumb, so he opened not his mouth" (Is. 50:6; 53:7). But it does not follow that one must proceed to regard him as a Kantian, i.e., that he acted in order that his behavior should be considered a universal law to be exacted upon everyone. It would be absurd to think so for that was the way of the scribes and the Pharisees: to turn everything into some inclusively binding precept.

This is not the free behavior of the saints. We are not all called to submit to be roasted over a fire like St. Laurence who, in the third century, refused to surrender to the Roman prefect the alms set aside for the poor of his parish. We are not all expected to renounce the world and go to live in caves in the wilderness as did Ss. Paul the Hermit, Antony the Abbot, Macarius, or Pambo; or stand naked before our Bishop and run off and preach to the Saracens as did St. Francis of Assisi. Nor are we all required to leave our country and live among the lepers as did Father Damien de Veuster of Molokai. Perhaps every Christian should deliberately seek martyrdom like the twenty-six who died at Nagasaki in the sixteenth century; or work among the poorest of the poor like St. Martin de Porres of Lima, Br. Charles de Foucauld of the Sahara, or Bl. Teresa of Calcutta?

We are not all called to these works of extraordinary holiness. Rather, for most of us the path is that of ordinary saints. The worth of our actions is fixed by the end they serve, and the greatest end any act can serve is the will of God. Grace perfects nature: it does not bind our wills, but sets us free to serve according to our circumstances and abilities. We act according as we are called to be in each and every moment. Therefore, let us not presume, for example, that we must universally become pacifists simply because Christ said: "offer no resistance to the wicked." Simple duty requires us to defend our loved ones from violent attack and, by extension, our country from war or invasion. Our duty to love and protect our family, for example, overrides the precept to suffer the enemy. It would be morally negligent to do so. To stand around passively before evil would render us complicit through inaction. Nevertheless, we are set free to choose to respond to any given evil with love and kindness. When it was a question of protecting his Father's house Christ would turn over the tables of the money changers. When it was a matter of defending the High Priest's servant, Jesus stayed Peter's hand and healed Malchus' severed ear. Our Lord is asking us to surpass the moral law, not to disobey it. If God so wills, certainly we can be called to heroic virtue, but that is not always the way.

> For everything there is a season, and a time for every
>   matter under Heaven:
> A time to be born, and a time to die,
> A time to plant, and a time to pluck up what is planted;
> A time to kill, and a time to heal;
> A time to break down and a time to build up;
> A time to weep, and a time to laugh;
> A time to mourn, and a time to dance;
>
> ...
>
> A time to rend, and a time to sew;
> A time to keep silence, and a time to speak;
> A time to love, and a time to hate;
> A time for war, and a time for peace.

And who is to judge the fruitfulness of the ordinary servant of God? Is it any the less heroic for a husband to labour long hours year after year in a factory or on a building site while patiently enduring some overbearing supervisor in order to provide for his wife and children? Do we regard as worthless the quiet and hidden sacrifice of the devoted wife and mother who nurtures her children while instilling in them the virtues of decency, holiness, and uprightness? Heroic not paltry are their responses to momentary slaps on the cheek, or daily sacrifices of time or possession, or being pressed to walk those extra miles. Such stalwart dedication of fathers and mothers serves to propagate the future citizens and formulators of the culture. Therein gestate the enduring contribution and latent potency of the people of God, for it is the nature of the kingdom to spread like yeast in dough. "Blessed are the meek for they shall inherit the earth."

> 43 You have heard how it was said, You will love your neighbour and hate your enemy. 44 But I say this to you, love your enemies and pray for those who persecute you; 45 so that you may be children of your Father in Heaven, for he causes his sun to rise on the bad as well as the good, and sends down rain to fall on the upright and the wicked alike. 46 For if you love those who love you, what reward will you get? Do not even the tax collectors do as much? 47 And if you save your greetings for your brothers, are you doing anything exceptional? 48 Do not even the gentiles do as much? You must therefore be perfect, just as your Heavenly Father is perfect.

If the law of retaliation led to a strict interpretation of justice then it is not surprising that there was controversy among the rabbis over Leviticus 19:18: "you shall not take vengeance, nor bear any grudge against the children of your people; you shall love your neighbour as yourself." On the one hand the *lex talionis* had enjoined equal repayment of justice, and on the other there was this command to love one's *neighbour*. Apparently this led to the conclusion on the part of the rabbis that while one ought to love one's neighbour—*"the children of your people"*—one should also hate Israel's enemies. This latter conclusion was arguable, since there were many verses in the Law and the Prophets that strongly indicated this, for example: "I will win glory for myself at the expense of Pharaoh and his army, chariots, and horsemen" (Ex. 14:17); "The LORD will be at war with Amalek generation after generation" (vs. 17:15); "See I am putting Sihon the Amorite, king of Heshbon, at your mercy, and his country too. Set about the conquest; engage him in battle. Today and henceforth, I shall fill the peoples under all Heaven with fear and terror of you" (Dt. 2:24–25); and "By this, you will know that the living God is with you and without doubt will expel the Canaanites, the Hittites, the Hivities, the Perizites, Girgashites, Amorites, and Jebusites before you" (Josh. 3:10).

These people were the enemies of Israel, and the Lord God had commanded their elimination. Did not the prophet Samuel berate king Saul for *not* having destroyed utterly the Amalekites?

> When YHWH sent you on a mission he said to you 'Go and put those sinners the Amelekites under the curse of destruction (*herem*) and make war on them until they are exterminated.' Why then did you not obey YHWH's voice? ... Since you have rejected YHWH's word, he has rejected you as king." (1 Sam. 15:18–23)

With examples like these there is no wonder that the rabbis should deduce that love for one's neighbour could not possibly be interpreted to include the wicked enemies of the people of God. Moreover, given Israel's history and the Lord's purpose regarding the elimination of the pagan nations—which would and indeed had corrupted all Israel leading eventually to their own destruction and exile—then the conclusion naturally follows: hate your enemies. "The fear of the LORD means hatred of evil" (Pr. 8:13). Was this not the constant command of the Lord of Hosts? Was this not the theme running through the Deuteronomy, Kings, and Chronicles, not to mention the psalms and the prophets? (See also for example Isaiah chapters 13–23; Amos 1–2; Habakkuk 2:6–20.) The entire Old Testament is suffused with the theme that God, himself, will inflict vengeance on Israel's enemies (See Dt. 32:35–41).

Thus on the one hand Israel was commanded to love their neighbour, but to retaliate in kind when wronged. And on the other they were directed to put their enemies under "the curse of destruction" and were promised by God that he also would requite vengeance against them. Of course, it must be understood that the original covenant with Israel included the promise of land subsequently inhabited by nations which not only practised idolatry, but also child sacrifice and temple prostitution. According to the Torah these peoples were to be overthrown in order to safeguard and preserve unpolluted the faith of Israel. "You are not going into their country to take possession because of any right behavior or uprightness on your part; rather, it is because of their wickedness that YHWH is dispossessing these nations for you, and also to keep the pact which he swore to your ancestors, Abraham, Isaac, and Jacob" (Dt. 9:5–6; also 18:9–12).

With such a ubiquitous and overwhelmingly obvious message it would have been startling for those assembled to hear Jesus say: "But I say this to you, love your enemies and pray for those who persecute you." And it is no wonder, since for the first time they were being introduced to an intimation of a New Covenant. The Old Covenant, which involved the nation of Israel, was now completed and is to be perfected in the Person of Christ. The following quotation makes this clear: "so that you may be children of your Father in Heaven, for he causes his sun to rise on the bad as well as the good, and sends down rain to fall on the upright and the wicked alike."

This is a sudden and disjunctive transition to an entirely new relationship centred upon Jesus himself. No longer are the people of God to be limited to a national loyalty based upon the kingdom of Israel or the temple at Jerusalem. Now they are the children of a Heavenly Father who causes his benevolence both to shine and to rain upon the upright and the wicked alike. Whereas the previous covenant required their survival and establishment as a national entity among the nations to prepare the way of the Lord (Mt. 3:3; Is. 40:3), the New Covenant has situated his people in an entirely new relationship with their Heavenly Father. Because their relationship is now to be centred upon the Son of God, their loyalties and obligations have been altered to those more characteristic of disciples, the followers of Jesus Christ. Therefore, their enemies are no longer the pagan nation states around them, for they are to go out into all the world making disciples from all nations (Mt. 28:19). Jesus' kingdom will be established among those who through faith in him become identified with him. Jesus himself is the centre and prince of this kingdom. They will then be persecuted simply because they proclaim him. "Blessed are you when people abuse you and persecute you . . . *on my account.*" The enemies have now changed, because with a change of centre, the entire periphery has been redrawn.

Of course, the Father was always the centre and the initiator of history. However, this history was not meant only for the sake of Israel as a political entity, but in order to prepare the way among all the nations for their Messiah. The people of God, having been chastised, were to be returned to their land only after having finally learned their lesson during the Exile (Dt. 28:36–57; 30:1–10). Now chastened, perhaps they learned it too well, for the national loyalties of the scribes, Pharisees, Sadducees, Zealots, and even the Essenes, blinded them to the interior meaning of the covenant, namely that their own Heavenly Father was the Father of all the other nations as well.

But with the coming of the Messiah, all that has been transcended. Jesus speaks of himself as the light of the world (Jn. 8:12) and his disciples too were also to become light (Mt. 5:14). Therefore, it is natural to accept the metaphor of sunlight shining on the wicked as well as the good as an illustration of how benevolently his disciples should behave. Similarly, the image of the rain that waters the just and the unjust, which carries all the allusions of baptism and grace that permeate the New Testament, also expresses the magnanimous charity Christians must pour upon the wicked. So when Jesus says to "love your enemies" not just those who will love in return; or to "pray for those who persecute you" and not just reserve your greetings for your brethren, he is simply asking his disciples to act as God acts. By resembling their Heavenly Father they are presenting themselves as his children, since children naturally image their fathers.

Thus Jesus' injunction to surpass the righteousness of the scribes and Pharisees requires more than merely avoiding hypocrisy: it is an invitation to conform oneself to the ethic of the kingdom of Heaven whereby even the moral law is surpassed. We have seen that it is perfectly moral to defend oneself and that it is ethically mandatory to protect the innocent against an unjust aggressor. For just as Israel inherited enemies as a result of their call, so we shall find ourselves subject to persecution also, and because of our call as well. The world will hate us, and our unruly flesh will rebel, and the devil will rage, but grace will triumph. "Rejoice and be glad, for your reward will be great in Heaven."

Our Lord was teaching that there is a higher law beyond the moral: the way of charity and compassion. So when a St. Francis, for example, could allow himself to be beaten and thrown into a snow-filled ditch, and even to suffer this with joy and laughter, we are given a profound illustration of an ethic which does not correspond to the way people normally think. Our usual reaction would be to seek reprisal against the perpetrator—and some would even deem it cowardly not to. But which is more courageous: to absorb the blows and respond with love, or to retaliate and "punch their lights out?" In the divine order of things the latter is weakness, while the former is sublime. "For my thoughts are not your thoughts, neither are your ways my ways, says the Lord. For as the Heavens are higher than the earth, so are my ways higher than your ways, and my thoughts than your thoughts" (Is. 55:8–9).

We have entered the kingdom through faith in Jesus Christ, who now reigns within us together with the Father and his Holy Spirit. God is constantly in act expressing his nature in the form of his Word and enacting his will through his Holy Spirit. Through faith in Christ Jesus the believer is caught up in this eternal action. Our faith unites us to Our Saviour. Our lives are grounded in him who lives in us. Slowly and inexorably we are sanctified, providing we do not frustrate or grieve the Spirit of God, or even, God forbid, commit the unpardonable sin of deliberately rejecting all help and grace. As long as we abide in Christ Jesus, we, like the sun-lit and rain-drenched earth, produce the fruits of virtue and holiness, wisdom and might, becoming more like the Son of the Father. Then we also come to be children of the Father, not by adoption merely, but through likeness, for we shall resemble the Son in grace and in truth. And then when God the Father looks upon us he will no longer see us, but his Son perfected within.

Therefore, we are perfected with the perfection of God; since we are incapable of such perfection on our own. From nothing comes nothing. So it is impossible for us to create virtue or produce holiness in ourselves. We cannot give ourselves what we lack. What is so obviously lacking in us must come from a higher source. Jesus had already promised that those who "hunger and thirst for righteousness will be filled." Such is the beatitude of the poor in spirit who know their need for God and who therefore ask, seek, and knock; for the Father in Heaven will assuredly give good things to those who ask him (Mt. 7:11). And Our Lord will assuredly "give what he commands," since he did not call us to perfection to mock us.

Yet this is not our own perfection, for we do not have it from ourselves. No, for Jesus asserts of his Father that it is *his* sun which rises and it is *he* who sends the rain. All things are in God's hands in a manner that goes deep down supporting the very substance of things. He forms our own substance also, for we too have our being in him. In him our cognition has its form and our will its principle of conation. We, who are made in the image of God from nothing, naturally share in his perfections, or else we have no reality, since all good things come from God. However, that special union which faith effects establishes a vital and deepening intimacy, because faith has joined us to that centre in our souls where Christ reigns, radiating his beauty. God's Truth is a living Spirit in whom we are invited to participate. Through submitting to his Spirit which animates our souls, we are enabled to evidence in our lives the fruit of supernatural virtue. With nothing to obstruct or hinder the Spirit, the whole person loves God and all his creatures with and in the very Spirit which proceeds from the Father and the Son. This is the Spirit of God moving over the face of the waters, stilling the waves, watering the valleys, renewing the face of the earth.

With such an abundance of grace bestowed upon you, then you will indeed surpass the law for you shall:

> Love your enemies, do good to those who hate you, bless those who curse you, pray for those who abuse you.... You will have a great reward, and you will be children of the Most High, for he himself is kind to the ungrateful and the wicked. Be merciful, even as your Father is merciful. (Luke 6:27, 35)

"Blessed are the merciful for they shall obtain mercy."

5

Living Prayer

O UR LORD has taught that our righteousness must exceed that of the scribes and Pharisees; and he has given us examples from scripture and rabbinic teaching to bring out how we are to distinguish ourselves from their practices. Moreover, this distinction requires that we become as perfect as God is perfect. Since such perfection is impossible from us by ourselves, then it is clear that such holiness can only come from God by the gracious action of his Holy Spirit. In this next part of his sermon Christ Jesus shows just how we may receive such grace.

He begins with the three pillars of Jewish piety: almsgiving, prayer, and fasting as illustrated in the book of Tobit: "Prayer with fasting and alms with uprightness are better than riches with iniquity" (12:8). In emphasizing these traditional practices which he assumes his disciples will perform—"*when* you give alms ... pray ... fast...."—Jesus again admonishes us to avoid hypocrisy and self-seeking so that these may be accomplished "with uprightness." Central to this section and, therefore, to the entire Sermon on the Mount is prayer where we are also given an example of the ideal prayer. Finally Our Saviour teaches us how to live constantly in prayerful communion with God.

6 ¹ Be careful not to parade your uprightness in public to attract attention; otherwise you will lose all reward from your Father in Heaven. ² So when you give alms, do not have it trumpeted before you; this is what the hypocrites do in the synagogues and in the streets to win human admiration. In truth I tell you, they have had their reward. ³ But when you give alms, your left hand must not know what your right is doing; ⁴ your almsgiving must be secret, and your Father who sees all that is done in secret will reward you.

Previously Jesus instructed us to let our light shine so that our Heavenly Father may be glorified. But we must never do it for the ulterior motive of winning the admiration of others. For this is what hypocrites do whose actions towards God are not sincere, but actually hide an inner duplicity. Inwardly they are lying to themselves, to others, and to God. They are deceiving themselves because they are corrupting the fundamental intention of the almsgiving, which should be done from a genuine motive of charity and for the benefit of the recipient. They are misleading others because they are promoting themselves and not the kingdom of Heaven. And they are lying to God, because it is not he who is being honoured. So that in setting their own glory above the glory of God, they are idolizing themselves and betraying irreverence for God. Moreover, their actions are not devoted singly and purely to God. For they are not pure in heart: and it is the pure in heart who will see God. And given that one reaps accordingly as one sows, then they will receive the reward they seek: human attention and that alone. Therefore, we should not imitate them since we also will lose any reward we might have otherwise received. In other words, the proper merits of the action will be obstructed, because we have ordered our intentionality to the world, and thereby have turned the soul's receptivity away from God.

The perfection to which Christ calls us is not something that can be obtained all at once, nor once and for all. It comes in degrees and can be lost in part. For perfection involves the growth in the virtues which are well described in Scripture and Tradition: these are the cardinal virtues of prudence, justice, temperance, and fortitude; the theological virtues of faith, hope, and charity; the evangelical virtues of poverty, chastity, and obedience; and the seven gifts of the Holy Spirit: wisdom, understanding, counsel, knowledge, piety, fortitude, and holy fear. All these virtues are operative principles which God implants within the soul and which enable us to perform meritorious acts. Little by little they act upon the intellect to enlighten it and upon the will to strengthen and form it so that virtue becomes ever more easy and habitual. The result is the proper formation of our character.

Thus as we perform charitable acts, pray, and practise self-control and denial we gradually detach ourselves from worldly things and become more open to Heavenly grace. We have observed that God is always in act giving each thing its own intelligible form. Everything receives proportionally according to its own limits from the infinite abundance of goodness which God, like the sun and the rain, disburses upon all of creation. It is the same with us. When we open to the plenitude which the Being of God constantly radiates, then we also receive from that infinite abundance. It is the nature of meritorious acts that they conform and transform us in such a way as to make us receptive to all that God has to give.

Herein lies a deep mystery about the disposition of the soul and its acquisition of divine grace. It is an unfathomable truth that the Eternal Being constantly acts in every quantum of reality. In every particle of our nature and in the least moment of our activity, God is mysteriously present sustaining our every expression and grounding each of its possibilities. "For God is the one working in you both to will and to work of his good pleasure" (Phil. 2:13). So the difficulty is not how we can get in touch with God's infinite operation, which acts everywhere, but rather how we fallen humans may desist from obstructing it. Thus, if we order our lives to the action of the Spirit which orders all things, including the secret motions of the heart, we cannot but help to receive all which he perfuses. It is like harmonizing oneself to a vast symphonic movement and then vibrating in concord with it. By attuning our every thought and action to accord with the nature which the Creator has placed in each thing, then we become part of this universal hymn to God. When we think aright our thoughts image the Word of God; and when we act aright our disposition accords with the Spirit of God. Goodness is diffusive of itself, so that by giving alms we are participating also in the divine self-giving and his love comes to be perfected in us.

The reward which alms receive is precisely the quality or character which any holy act by its nature confers upon those who are justified and in a state of grace. This is known as condign merit (*meritum de condigno*), or merit from worth. Charitable works obtain for us this merit by virtue of the fact that they are ordered to God and come from God. They flow from divine grace itself to the person who is in a state of grace; i.e., to one who is participating in the life of God. Such actions are beautiful in themselves and are worthy of reward. It is the divine action that gives them this perfection.

One may also receive a merit of congruity (*meritum de congruo*) even if the work should only be ordered to uprightness. This sort of work flows from actual graces already present in a person which dispose one to receive grace for oneself or for another. These merits solely come from the harmony or congruity of a person's friendship or closeness with God—such as that of the saints in Heaven who, because of their state of friendship or nearness to God, can intercede for us.

The fundamental difference between the two is that in condign merit the reward is due to us from justice, because God has promised to reward such a good work performed in him and for love of him. God has ordained things to this end. For him not to have rendered what is duly deserved would have been unjust. An example of condign merit is given in the parable of the hired labourers in the vineyard (Mt. 20:1–16) who were promised a fixed reward for their works. Through their contracted labour, their works justly merited the agreed wage.

It is different with congruent merit where the reward is freely given from kindness. God bestows it in appreciation of the work done by that person who is in a state of friendship with him. The reward is, as it were, optional and gratuitous, so that to refuse to give it would not be unjust. An example of congruent merit is given by the parable of the publican (Lk. 18:9–14) who, unlike the self-righteous Pharisee, received justification through his humble and contrite appeal to God. God did not have to give him this grace *because* of justice, for it was not owed to the sinful publican since he had no rightful claim upon it. God did so liberally out of his benevolent and abundant mercy.

God has decreed the nature of things to be such that alms done in the right disposition and for the proper motives will ordinarily receive merit in proportion to the loving faith of the disciple. The more spontaneous and ingenuous the action, the less obstructive it is to grace. The more the soul's intention is ordered to God, the more his Spirit can operate within. With all one's affections conformed to his Spirit, every action becomes holy through participation. Suffused with grace, the soul becomes more and more absorbed in God. This is what Our Lord meant by not letting one's left hand (symbolizing the intellect) know what the right hand (or the will) is doing. Since there is no longer anything to impede God's will, the soul cannot distinguish anything in herself which is not from God. For then all her activity arises within that secret place of the heart, "hid with Christ in God," where one's will is one substance with the divine action. "And your Father who sees all that is done in secret will reward you."

> And when you pray, do not imitate the hypocrites: they love to say their prayers standing up in the synagogues and at the street corners for people to see them. In truth I tell you, they have had their reward. ⁶ But when you pray, go to your private room, shut yourself in, and so pray to your Father who is in that secret place, and your Father who sees all that is done in secret will reward you. ⁷ In your prayers do not babble as the gentiles do, for they think that by using many words they will make themselves heard. ⁸ Do not be like them; your Father knows what you need before you ask him.

By the giving of alms, of course, was meant all charitable actions directed to others. But there is a supreme action which is ordered to God, and that is prayer. Prayer (*tefillah*) is the second of the works of piety which Jews were expected to perform. Ordinarily they were accustomed to pray the *Shema* (Dt. 6:4–9) morning and evening, while putting on the phylacteries, as well as the *Amidah* or Eighteen Benedictions three times a day. Prayers were also offered at the beginning and end of every meal, at special events, and on various occasions such as: when seeing an impressive city, upon glimpsing the beauty of nature, at weddings and other occasions of rejoicing, when answering the call of nature, when entering and leaving one's home (the *mezuzah*), upon seeing physical deformity, etc. Indeed almost every aspect of daily life had some prayer associated with it. Prayer was a natural part of the pious Jew's daily round. The Synagogue was the focus of prayer in most villages and towns particularly on the Sabbath, while the Temple of Jerusalem was the national centre of the Jewish life of worship during the many prescribed sacrificial feasts, especially *Pesach* and *Yom Kippur*.

Once again Jesus requires that the motives must be pure and single, from love of God, and performed with sincerity. One must not imitate those hypocrites who like to display their piety—which, of course, is a fault not just restricted to a few first century Jews. Nevertheless, as with hypocrisy in almsgiving, Our Lord condemns the practice, warning that they already have their reward: i.e., that they cannot expect to receive a divine blessing when what they really desired was to seek admiration from others. How could they when their attitude betrayed such a casual and even flippant disregard of the majesty of the One to whom they were pretending to pray?

In contrast to such an ostentatious and shallow display of prayer, Our Lord advises that "when you pray you must enter your private room, shut yourself in, and so pray to your Father who is in that secret place." Obviously, a literal, physical understanding of these words cannot be intended here, for that would put one in the position of having to avoid all prayers in public. The absurdity and awkwardness of carrying out such an interpretation, given all the commandments in the Torah regarding festivals and days of obligation, clearly indicate that Jesus means for his hearers to take his meaning in a spiritual sense. All prayer, whether public or private, must be a holy and intimate affair between the believer and one's God. The God and Father of us all, who abides in the "secret place," deserves to be approached with reverence and devotion. Therefore, to "enter one's private room and to close oneself in" means that prayer to God should arise from deep within one's soul, in that secret holy place where our Father dwells.

Prayer is that sacred act whereby the soul enters into a direct communion with God. To describe prayer as a sacred act is only to emphasize that this communion links the most intimate part of the soul with the Father; because the union is made at that point where God operates within the soul, loving it into being. Even if the prayer in itself is not, in a given moment, so deep, nevertheless, that point of mutual touching is precisely where our reality is constantly borne in the substance of God. To be sure, the "Spirit also comes to help us in our weakness, for, when we do not know how to pray properly, then the Spirit personally supplicates for us in inexpressible groanings" (Ro. 8–26). Thus even public prayer remains private if it is genuinely offered. The Lord gently urges us to pray sincerely from deep within the cloister of our soul so that the sanctity of this earnest communion may be safeguarded.

That is why heaping up empty phrases is so brash and presumptive. To dare to explain our needs to God in never ending, artificially manufactured phrases only serves to insult the awe and majesty of his presence. In a sense it even denies it: for it disdains his omniscience. Of course, God knows what we need, so that he ordinarily bestows upon us innumerable benefits which are unasked, even unsought. "Even before they call I shall answer; while they are still speaking, I shall have heard" (Is. 65:24). But there are some things that God wants us to ask of him for our own sake, that we may increase our confidence in him and graciously thank him as the source of all good things. Our Heavenly Father is pleased with our requests and delighted to help us, but all he requires is simple petition so that we may grow in faith when our prayers are answered; or so as to strengthen our trust and resignation when it is his will not to grant a particular request.

For our God is not like the gods of the pagans who had to be placated and convinced to come to their aid over against some other more vindictive gods who may be in opposition to them. This can never be the case with the one only God whose immensity and power extend to every part of creation. The essential characteristic of God—his infinity of Being, i.e., his Reality in act—accounts for all his properties: his oneness, truth, goodness, and beauty; his omniscience, omnipotence, and omnipresence; as well as simplicity of substance, since there are no parts to delimit him.[1] For what is unlimited includes all possible being and all possible perfection. God lacks nothing and there is nothing which is impossible for him. "Hear, O Israel! YHWH is our God, the LORD is one. Therefore,

---

1. The reason is that all other properties—omniscience, goodness, simplicity, etc.—admit of degrees, so that it is also possible to predicate these properties univocally of creatures, albeit in an analogically proportional manner; whereas actual infinity can only be predicated categorematically of God. Moreover infinity of being includes all other possible perfections. See Bl. John Duns Scotus, *Philosophical Writings*, tr. Allan Wolter (Cambridge: Hackett Publishing Co., 1987), p.27.

you shall love the LORD with all your heart, and with all your soul, and with all your strength" (Dt. 6: 4–5).

⁹ So you should pray like this: Our Father in Heaven, may your name be held holy,
¹⁰ your kingdom come, your will be done, on earth as in Heaven.
¹¹ Give us today our daily bread.
¹² And forgive us our debts, as we have forgiven those who are in debt to us.
¹³ And do not put us to the test, but save us from the Evil One.
¹⁴ Yes, if you forgive others their failings, your Heavenly Father will forgive you yours; ¹⁵ but if you do not forgive others, your Father will not forgive your failings either.

At the time of Jesus many Jewish prayers already included some form of the words: "*Baruch atah Adonai eloheinu melech ha'olam*" or "Blessed are you, Lord our God, king of creation." Examples of these customary blessings were recorded in the late first-century *Mishnah Berakhot* which dealt, among other things, with rulings covering a number of occasional prayers. For example, when putting on the phylacteries a Jew was required to say: "Blessed are you, Lord our God, king of creation, who has sanctified us with His commandments and has commanded us to put on *tefillin*." When blessing bread or wine, the following would be said: "Blessed are you, etc., who brings forth bread from the earth." or "Blessed are you, etc., who creates the fruit of the vine."

Our Lord's Prayer comprises a form of this traditional blessing, although Jesus has rearranged its elements somewhat. Thus "our God," *eloheinu*, is placed first for emphasis and is made much more personal by addressing our God as Our *Father*. The phrase "blessed are you, Lord" thus becomes the first petition: "hallowed be your *name*." Here "name" refers to the Tetragrammaton (YHWH), which was held to be far too sacred to pronounce. Jesus then expands "king of creation" into "your kingdom come, your will be done" by altering the phrase into two more petitions. As a result, these first three petitions mirror, as it were, the first tablet of the Ten Commandments. Similarly, the remaining four supplications of the prayer concern one's personal holiness, just as the second tablet does.

Our Father in Heaven. All things have been entrusted to Jesus Christ by his Heavenly Father "and no one knows the Son except the Father, just as no one knows the Father except the Son and those to whom the Son chooses to reveal him" (Mt. 11:27). In the opening words of Our Lord's Prayer, Jesus does indeed reveal to us the fatherhood of God which is made available to we who "believe in his name" and "who are guided by the Spirit of God . . . the Spirit of adoption, which enables us to exclaim, *Abba,* Father!" And because we are no longer slaves to the sins of this world, we are "sons and daughters," therefore, heirs, "by God's own act" for no one comes to the Son unless drawn by the Father. Therefore, since we are already God's children, "when he appears we shall be like him for then we shall see him as he is."[2]

Our Blessed Lord and Saviour, Jesus Christ, comes in the name of the Father with the purpose of revealing him to us as the One who is immanent in the Son, and who through our adoption brings us into the same intimate relationship with the Father as that of the Son:

> May they all be one, just as, Father, you are in me and I am in you, so that they also may be in us, so that the world may believe it was you who sent me, I have given them the glory you gave to me, that they may be one as we are one. With me in them and you in me, may they be so perfected in unity that the world will recognise that it was you who sent me and that you have loved them as you have loved me. (Jn. 17: 21–22)

Therefore, the Father is intimately near to all his children and wants them to approach him with confidence, trusting in his infinite mercy and goodness. There should be no grounds for fear or trepidation, for we can run to him with the abandonment and liberty of little children who happily cry *Abba* or "Papa." There is nothing which you cannot ask of him, for he loves you and wants to give good things to you.

Having been set free from the stain of original sin through the waters of baptism, we are now heirs to the promise of eternal life providing we persevere in keeping his commandments. Being heirs to his

---

2. Jn. 1:12; Ro.8:14–17; Gal. 4:6; 2 Cor. 6:18; Jn. 6: 44; 1 Jn. 3: 1–2.

kingdom, we are also enabled to move towards perfection so that we may become more Christ-like, conformed more and more perfectly to the image of the Son; for we have received that Spirit of adoption who communicates the Son within us. Caught up in the love of the Son for the Father and the Father for the Son, which is in us through this Spirit, we come to know the beauty of the Son who radiates from within. Just as the Son images the Father upon whom he lovingly looks, so we are perfected thereby and come to be like him.

Moreover, he is our Father in *Heaven* (literally "in the Heavens"). That is, he is the creator and sustainer of all that is. For just as it is possible geometrically to project all of space and time from a single point, so it is with God who, as in a point, dwells in all things, for he is limited by no spatial or temporal dimensions. God acts everywhere; yet he is localized to no particular space or time. Rather God dwells in that deep mystery which is his Heavenly place, where he reigns in majesty. So we must approach him with due reverence and awe, but also with supreme trust and confidence in the one who holds all things in his hand.

Although Heaven is his dwelling place—and, through his Son, his Heaven is within us as well—nevertheless, he wants us to be there with him, "that they may always see my glory which you have given me because you have loved me before the foundation of the world" (Jn. 17:24). This is the beatific vision of the Son in the Father in the love of the Holy Spirit: a vision to which we are heirs providing we remain in Christ Jesus, who brings with him the kingdom of Heaven.

Hallowed be thy name. How can one express the holiness of God whose name must not even be pronounced: the One who is, before whom even the fiery ones, the Seraphim, can only approach with their faces covered by their wings? "Holy, holy, holy is the LORD God of Hosts: the whole earth is filled with his glory" (Is. 6:3).

> His glory covers the Heavens,
> and the earth is filled with his praise.
> His splendour is like the day.
> Rays beam from beside him,
> where his power is hid. (Hab. 3:3–4)

God's name is holy because it discloses an identity which is demarcated from all which is evil. This follows naturally from his infinity and immensity which can admit neither privation nor stain of perfection. God's infinite nature is inconsistent with any defect. Thus God dwells in impenetrable light. This is reflected in the name which God revealed to Moses from the burning bush: "I am who I am" or "I am that is." English cannot adequately bring out the meaning of the Hebrew. The Scholastic Doctors usually explain the phrase by saying God is Being in act. By this they mean that God is an absolute plenitude of perfection which pours forth from his unbounded Reality; or, if you will, the Being that radiates being in all its fruitful abundance. But such words fail before the presence of God. Moses was not allowed to see God's face. The Seraphim, as pure as fire, are themselves humbled by the utter exclusiveness of God's effulgent perfection. "God is terrible in the assembly of the holy ones; he is great and dreaded among all who surround him" (Ps. 89:7). Nothing unholy can approach the Holy One of Israel. Therefore, "Depart from me, for I am a sinful man" (Lk. 5:8).

But "blessed are the pure in heart, for they shall see God." What more majestic revelation can we have of the extraordinary redemption offered to those who truly believe and confess that Jesus is Lord! What greater statement can be given of the reality of the kingdom effected within us when Our Lord comes to dwell in us and we in him! Can we not see that there is a holy and sacred centre in every believer? "Do you not realize that you are the temple of the Holy Spirit with the Spirit of God living in you?" (1 Cor. 3:16; cf. 2 Cor. 6:16–18.)

Since God lives in every believer it follows that when we pray we should consciously place ourselves in his presence by reminding ourselves that "the ground on which we stand is holy ground." Enter into your secret oratory where God dwells within and find him there in the silent meditations of your heart, by making a deliberate intention to exclude everything sensible that does not lead to God. "When you pray go into the secret room, and shut the door."

Then we shall be able to extend prayer into our everyday actions as well, by also offering to him beforehand all that we are about to do, and afterwards giving thanks to him when we have done; so that in this continual communion, "we are also employed in praising, adoring, and loving him unceasingly, for his infinite goodness and perfection."[3] Slowly we shall come to realize that we are never far from his loving presence. When we at last come to understand that God is truly present to us in every moment, then everything we do or offer before him becomes a prayer which hallows his name.

Thus, there is neither art nor science to knowing God. As though he were not already within us! We need only act believing that God is always with us—that he is closer than the pulsations of our hearts—and "it shall be done to you according to your faith" (Mt. 9:29). Our unmerited gift of faith is the proximate means for attaining to God, since "faith is the substance of things hoped for, the evidence of things not seen" (Heb. 1:11). To persevere in faith only requires that we place ourselves in God's presence by directing our hearts to nothing but him, to do all for his sake, and to love him unceasingly above all things.

Yet it is the prayer of Our Lord that the name of God be hallowed *on earth*, since it is intended to be understood that all three petitions are to be governed by the summative clause: "on earth as it is in Heaven."[4] It then follows that we must cultivate the virtues, free ourselves from all falsehood, so that no one is scandalized by our behavior, and "we should wash ourselves clean of everything that pollutes either body or spirit, bringing our sanctification to completion in the fear of God" (2 Cor. 7:1).

Thy kingdom come. We have just been describing the kingdom of Heaven within us, but it *is* to have an earthly dimension as well. Indeed, it cannot fail to do so, since as the kingdom spreads from believer to believer, so its moral, cultural, and social effects spread throughout the world like a mustard seed which becomes a great tree. That tree is the catholic faith which comprises the Church militant on earth and the Church triumphant in Heaven. By praying for

---

3. Br. Lawrence (Nicholas Herman of Lorraine), *The Practice of the Presence of God*, fourth conversation.

4. *Catechism of the Council of Trent*, p. 514.

the coming of the kingdom on earth as in Heaven, we are asking that the Heavenly reign of Christ be realized here on earth also. Ultimately it will be realized in his final coming when he returns to institute his eternal kingdom. Hence the book of Revelations ends its magnificent and portentous drama of salvation history with the invocation *marana tha*, "Come, Lord Jesus." But his kingdom is to a degree already being established here on earth, although amid much opposition and persecution.

Even so, for those poor in spirit who know their need for God, "the kingdom of Heaven is theirs." For genuinely to yearn for the coming of Christ's reign on earth already presupposes that one possesses that faith in he who brings the kingdom to all who believe in his name. Therefore, the *anawim*, the blessed people of God, are asked also to pray for the coming of the kingdom *on earth* as it is in Heaven. God governs the universe with power and with providence. In God's hands are the ends of the earth and its hidden depths. Our prayer, then, presupposes the fulfilment of those things which lie concealed in the deepest recesses of creation. And in our hearts as well! But it is also clear that the kingdom of this world belongs to the evil one, the father of lies and the prince of darkness. Therefore, to pray for the coming of the kingdom is finally to pray for the continued curtailment of evil's influence over people's hearts, and for the devil's decisive casting out. It is to pray that truth and justice be realized in our nation and in the world, for "the kingdom of God is justice and peace and joy in the Holy Ghost" (Ro. 14:17).

Thy will be done on earth as it is in Heaven. The saints and Doctors of the Church all teach that nothing is done apart from God's will. Thus, St. Basil the Great teaches that: "Whatever has come to pass has come to pass by the will of our Creator. And who can resist God's will? Let us accept what has befallen us; for if we take it ill we do not mend the past and we work our own ruin. Do not let us arraign the righteous judgment of God."[5] St. John Chrysostom also agrees: "if any of the events which happen pass our understanding, let us not from this consider that our affairs are not gov-

5. Letter 6:2.

erned by providence, but perceiving His providence in part, in things incomprehensible let us yield to the unsearchableness of His wisdom."[6] This is also the position of St. Augustine which summarizes the sentiments of *De Genesis ad Litteram* that:

> All that happens to us in this world against our will (whether due to men or to other causes) happens to us only by the will of God, by the disposal of Providence, by His orders and under His guidance; and if from the frailty of our understanding we cannot grasp the reason for some event, let us attribute it to divine Providence, show Him respect by accepting it from His hand, and believe firmly that He does not send it us without cause.[7]

Indeed, this is one of the most solidly established and most consoling of the truths that have been revealed to us in both Scripture and Tradition that nothing happens to us in life unless God wills it so.[8]

If it is the case that by his providence God protects and governs all things which he has made, then why are we required to pray that his will be done if all things happen according to God's will anyway? Yet nature operates according to its own laws and human beings have been given free will, so that the whole complex of creation, having been established in this manner, entails that God has foreordained the cooperation of his creatures. That is what creation is: a system of laws and principles all designed for particular ends. God can use these secondary causes in order to accomplish his greater purpose.

Human beings are also given the opportunity and dignity to cooperate in God's eternal plan. Of course, fallen human nature has engendered structures, institutions, and events which are contrary to God's deliberate will. Yet even these can be used by the almighty

6. *That Demons do not Govern this World,* Homily II.

7. Quoted in Fr. Baptiste Saint-Jure, *The Knowledge and Love of Our Lord Jesus Christ* (Rockford: Tan, 1983), p. 17.

8. Bl. Claude de la Colombiere, *Trustful Surrender to Divine Providence,* (Rockford: Tan, 1983), p. 95. This is confirmed by Vatican I: "God protects and governs all things which he has made, 'reaching mightily from one end of the earth to the other, and ordering all things sweetly' (Wis. 8:1). For 'all are open and laid bare to his eyes' (Heb. 4:13), even those things which are yet to come into existence through the free action of creatures." (Dz. 1784) See also *CCC* 303 ff.

God, through his permissive will, to bring about even greater good. They do not limit God's power, nor do they make him dependent upon them, for all is foreseen by God from eternity. Even our prayers are foreknown by him. Having already been encouraged to pray for the coming of God's kingdom, we are now asked to pray for the acceptance of God's will: it is a prayer of resignation. And it is this resignation or acceptance of God's will in all things without complaint that will sanctify us.

Whatever is in the power of our wills and our means we may accomplish with God's help; but what is beyond us must be accepted with resignation, even with joy, for it is God's will. It is his word spoken to us through the surface appearance of circumstances. Here is our opportunity to express our faith and love for God by saying "Thy will be done." For herein lie our faith, martyrdom, self-denial, and obedience: that we love God in all our circumstances. What greater conformity can we have to the mind and will of God than to place ourselves in his loving hands by obediently accepting his disciplines and chastisements, and his consolations? Since he knows what is best for us, when we happily accept his will in this present moment and circumstance, and thank him for it, are we not making a heroic act of virtue? It is easy to love God when all is going well, but to love him in the midst of misfortune or persecution is surely the greatest virtue.

Once again, it is not necessary to go out of our way to seek for extraordinary means of holiness, for God gives us in each moment the opportunity to serve him in this manner. To recognize that all things are ultimately in his hands is a supreme expression of faith to be sure. But the deeper reality is that we are always in the presence of God. How could it be otherwise? If this moment is as God wills it to be—and it is impossible from his infinity and immensity that this is not so—then it follows that there is never an instant when God is not present to us. Where God acts, there he is. By willing this moment and faithfully acknowledging his will, we enter into his presence: for God is not only here now by his eternal act, but he is also in your will, making it possible, and in your soul, giving it form. "Therefore, I am content with weaknesses, insults, hardships, persecutions, and constraints, for the sake of Christ; for it is when I am weak, that I am strong" (2 Cor. 12:10). "Blessed are the meek, for they shall have the earth for their inheritance."

Give us this day our daily bread. We have prayed for the sanctification of the name of God; that his kingdom be realized; and that his will be accepted. These three petitions formed the first tablet of Our Lord's Prayer: the things that pertain to God. The next four petitions concern our own worldly estate: the preservation of our physical and moral life as well as our psychological and spiritual well-being.

To move from the rarefied atmosphere of seeking the presence of God in all things, to asking for our daily sustenance, seems at first sight to be something of a descent. The words "give us" clearly express our childlike dependency upon Our Heavenly Father, since there is nothing we have which does not come from God. Furthermore, the words "daily bread" intend more than literal bread, but everything else that is necessary for our existence as well. This petition already presupposes that trust which comes from an ardent faith which has been expressed in the first three petitions: that the one holy God is Lord and sustainer of all existence and we are his creatures. Therefore, it is not unnatural to ask for even the merest of things, since before God, we are all beggars, and God knows we have need of these things.

The kingdom of God is an immanent fact and a dynamic reality. Everything we seek and receive ought to be understood by the faithful as occurring within the kingdom of God. So when we come to note that the Greek word *epiousion* rendered "daily bread" can also mean in English (via Latin) "super-essential" bread, we are yet again elevated to other more spiritual considerations. Bread which is super-essential is clearly bread which is basic to our sustenance—hence the translation "daily"—since it is always necessary for us. So the first thing is to pray not only for things which are basic to our sustenance, but also to intercede for those people who lack even these necessities of life.

Of course, this also immediately reminds us of the Blessed Sacrament which Our Lord declared to be his body and blood. However, although the desire for daily communion of the sacrament is not to be disrespected, nevertheless, it is neither always possible nor practical: not for many of us in the world, neither for the desert fathers, nor for the sick and housebound, etc. Certainly, it is proper and fitting to seek to communicate daily, but we must not turn this petition into a precept.

Hence, St. Augustine, noting these points, detects a third spiritual meaning: "that is to say, divine precepts, which we ought daily to meditate and to labour after." Just as bread is necessary for nourishment, as well as the visible sacramental host, so also do we require "the invisible bread of the word of God." According to this interpretation, the soul that is impoverished, deluded, or sickened by worldly lies, errors, and vanities needs the correction and illumination that only the word of God can give. In this case, to pray for our daily bread is to ask that we be constantly illuminated and refreshed by meditating on the truths and precepts given us in Scripture and Tradition. It is also to pray for those in the world who hunger for the truth, that they may be filled.

Yet there is another sense which accords with all that we have said before: *viz.* that mystical Heavenly banquet to which we are all ultimately called. Who *is* this Jesus who brings with him the kingdom; who makes the kingdom a living reality in those who place their faith in him; who draws life from the Father and who feeds us with the bread of life; and who raises us up on the last day to feast with him forever in his eternal place? Is it not the same Jesus who said:

> In all truth I tell you, it was not Moses who gave you the bread from Heaven, it is my Father who gives you the bread from Heaven, the true bread; for the bread of God is the bread which comes down from Heaven and gives life to the world. . . . I am the bread of life. No one who comes to me will ever hunger; no one who believes in me will ever thirst. . . . It is my Father's will that whoever sees the Son and believes in him should have eternal life, and that I should raise him up on the last day. (Jn. 6: 32–40, *passim*)

Few among the saints are those who have received mystical communion with the Lord. Ss. Catherine of Sienna, Francis of Assisi, Teresa of Avila, John of the Cross, Elizabeth of the Trinity, and Pio of Pietrelcina immediately spring to mind. This is an extremely high union commonly referred to as the spiritual marriage; and is only possible for those who have, as it were, stripped their souls of all that would impede their union with Christ. "Blessed are those who hunger and thirst for righteousness, for they shall be satisfied." Even so, it is this same Jesus who dwells within the soul of every believer, who radiates all grace and goodness into our souls through His Holy Spirit, and who forms us into one mystical body with him. The petition for daily bread extends also to the request for this super-substantial sustenance from Our Blessed Lord and Saviour who imparts his own eternal life to whoever believes in him. "With me in them and you in me, may they be so perfected in unity that the world will recognize that it was you who sent me and that you have loved them as you have loved me" (Jn. 17:23).

Forgive us our trespasses, as we forgive those who have trespassed against us. Matthew has the Greek word for "debts" in both instances, whereas Luke has "sins" in the first instance and "debts" in the second. Nevertheless, it makes no difference since it is generally understood that offences against God are meant in the first and offences against us in the second. And that is the meaning in Matthew as well, since the injunction to forgive others is repeated at the end of the prayer. Therefore, the meaning is straightforward: "if you forgive others their failings, your Heavenly Father will forgive you yours; but if you do not forgive others, your Father will not forgive your failings either."

Jesus had implied this earlier in his sermon with regard to becoming reconciled with one's adversary before making one's offering at the altar. (The reader will recall that this was in the context of surpassing the righteousness of the Pharisees.) However, there is more to this petition for forgiveness than the mere issue of hypocrisy: for it is not simply a matter of personal unseemliness or inconsistency. Once again we are being exhorted to live and act in harmony with the ethos of the kingdom. If we do not forgive others, then we offend against mercy, and we place ourselves in peril of grave sin, i.e., we may extinguish the life of grace in us. Consequently, we shall have separated ourselves from God's mercy; and we shall no longer be living in the presence of God.

It is not God who has moved, but we who have done so, by our deliberate act of disbelieving a truth: *viz.* that the kingdom of God is received by grace through faith. Especially so, for in denying this truth we are denying Jesus who is the embodiment of this truth. We ourselves have received forgiveness by virtue of our faith in Christ Jesus, which faith presupposes the acceptance of all that he intends for us. But this faith is an unmerited gift of mercy given us by our Heavenly Father. Our act of refusing forgiveness to others is a betrayal of this mercy and an offense against God. It places us in a state of untruth, of bad faith; and it erects an obstacle to the flow of grace into us. If we do not have the predisposition to forgive, to show mercy, then we are not of the kingdom. We do not have the mind of Christ.

Life in God is one life, for we are one with him in his Holy Spirit. The action of this Spirit is love and the expression of love directed towards sinners is mercy. The apostle of mercy, St. Faustina Kowalska, has said: "We resemble God most when we forgive our neighbours. God is love, Goodness, and Mercy…

> Every soul, and especially the soul of every religious, should reflect My mercy. My Heart overflows with compassion and mercy for all. The heart of my beloved must resemble Mine; from her heart must spring the fountain of My mercy for souls; otherwise I will not acknowledge her as Mine.[9]

Mercy is the disposition of the Christ who came into the world to redeem it by his passion, death, and resurrection. The cross is the fount of mercy and the purpose of Christ's incarnation: "When you have lifted up the Son of man, then you will know that I AM, and that I do nothing of my own accord, but I say only what my Father taught me" (Jn. 8:28). This "lifting up" is a clear reference to the cross and not to his resurrection, since Jesus is saying to his persecutors "when *you* have lifted up the Son of man. . . ." It is at that moment of supreme sacrifice that Jesus will be known by his sacred name: I AM. The crucifixion reveals Christ as the One Who Is because he is God giving his life for us. God is the Being who gives

9. *Diary,* no. 1148.

being; and the gift of the Son of God is his flesh. He is the super-essential bread of life for which we have just been asked to pray. But we cannot feed at this altar unless we are prepared to live out the life of mercy which is being poured out for us. We too must become mercy, for we have been called by mercy to give mercy. It is thus that we become identified with Christ as we become one with him *in* his merciful love.

Moreover, Christ is the Word of God and, therefore, his redemptive coming into the world was fundamentally an expression of God's merciful love. In fact, the character of Christ's saving action expresses that love by which the Father generates the Son and by which the Son glorifies the Father: "I say only what my Father taught me." For this Holy Spirit of love is just the life of the Holy Trinity who also lives in us and sanctifies us. It is by the cross of Christ that we have been set free from our sins and are entitled to the inheritance of his kingdom. But this kingdom is a life and an ethos which we must also express by displaying the same mercy and forgiveness to others. "Blessed are the merciful, for they shall obtain mercy."

And lead us not into temptation. In his instructions and in the prayer which Our Blessed Lord is conveying to us, we have been brought ever more deeply into an understanding of the kingdom of Heaven. Far surpassing the righteousness of those who would manipulate the kingdom for their own ends or who would reduce it to something more mundane and manageable—and less confrontational, thereby—Jesus desires that we abide in his love, which is *the* formative principle of the kingdom.

> Abide in me as I in you. As a branch cannot bear fruit all by itself unless it remains part of the vine, neither can you unless you remain in me. I am the vine, you are the braches. Whoever abides in me, with me in him, bears abundant fruit; for cut off from me you can do nothing. . . . I have loved you just as the Father has loved me. Remain in my love." (Jn. 15: 4–5, 9)

This love cannot be separated from His Person, nor from the other Persons of the Triune God.

The love of God, when considered from the perspective of creatures, is mercy, as we have seen; and we are closest to the kingdom of God when mercy also informs our sentiments toward others. But a constant threat against the presence of God's kingdom in us is temptation since: "anyone who does not remain in me is thrown away like a branch—and withers" (vs. 6). Therefore, Jesus enjoins us to pray that we are not led or brought to the test, lest we too suffer the withering of his life in us. The Greek word *peirasmos*, usually translated temptation, is better rendered "trial" or "test."[10] Otherwise, the word "temptation" would contradict our sense of religious propriety, not to mention the ontological fact, that God is never the author of evil. This is borne out in James 1:13: "Let no one say when one is tempted, 'I am tempted of God;' for God cannot be tempted with evil, neither does he tempt anyone." When, therefore, we speak of being brought to the test we are clearly speaking of the permissive will of God, rather than his deliberate will.

Now the traditional sources of temptation are the world, the flesh, and the devil (the evil one). We shall have an opportunity to say something on the last source of temptation, evil itself, when we consider the next petition, "deliver us from evil." Here we shall restrict ourselves to the first two: our fallen culture and our weakened flesh. Both of these are subordinated to the providence of God, insofar as God has permitted the fall, and by implication all that has flowed from it down the course of the centuries. In these latter times we are witnessing the demise of Christian culture throughout the entire world. The rise of secularism in the West and the usurpation of the religion of Mohammed by militant fundamentalists throughout the East are all too apparent. These rebellions have resulted in great pressures to conform to the dominant ideology of their respective cultures—even including out and out persecutions against those who would not capitulate. Here the hostility to the teachings of Jesus has become all too plainly manifested to us.

It is in fact shocking that even Christians would ever consider questioning Our Lord's clear precepts and wisdom. But in almost every area of modern life this is a lamentable occurrence among not

10. Cf. Walter Bauer et al., *A Greek-English Lexicon of the New Testament and Other Early Christian Literature* (Chicago: Universtiy of Chicago Press, 1979), ad locum.

a few Christians as well. However, they have no demonstrable excuse for their apostasy—there is no other word for that rejection of the teachings of the Son of God which is becoming so evident today. Here the trial and testing weighs heavily upon the people of God: hence the need to pray for strength and light to enable us to resist such temptations to depart from the kingdom.

This petition, to be preserved from the trials and temptations of contemporary culture, is thus a prayer for the curtailment of its influence on us and others. Jesus warned that there would be times of testing for Christians, and there have been throughout the course of history many eras of torment and anguish for the Church. Furthermore, it is the teaching of Christ and his Church that the end times in particular would be manifested by extreme tribulation for all believers.

The second source of temptation after the world is the flesh, i.e., the desires and tendencies of the heart. In this regard we happily attend to the words of Our Lord:

> Hear me, all of you, and understand: there is nothing outside a man which by entering into him can defile him; but the things which come out of a man are what defile him. . . . For from within, out of the heart of man, come evil thoughts, fornication, theft, murder, adultery, coveting, wickedness, deceit, licentiousness, envy, slander, pride, foolishness. All these evil things come from within, and they defile a man. (Mk. 7:16, 20–23)

Thus, however prevalent the cultural influences to evil, they do not constitute sin unless and until they are acted upon. Sin only becomes such when it is a deliberate and free act of the will which involves matter which is in itself morally wrong. We all have inherent disordered tendencies and weaknesses as a result of our fallen nature, and we are particularly vulnerable to suggestions from the world, but these do not constitute sin until they enter the will.

This clearly presupposes that humans have free will. Indeed, that we do have free will can be taken as axiomatic from Jesus' own teachings: otherwise his reproval of sin, his excoriation of the hypocrisy of the scribes and the Pharisees, his exhortation to obey his commandments, and his warnings of damnation and his promises of eternal life to those who seek it, would lack justification. It would make no sense for Our Lord to require the woman taken in adultery to "Go and sin no more," to ask the rich young ruler to sell his possessions, or to interrogate the authenticity of St. Peter's love, if Jesus did not expect the free response of every individual to accede to his word.

Therefore, because we have free will, no one can claim a special exemption proffering one's disordered, fallen nature as an excuse. We are not mere animals driven by instincts and desires we cannot control: we are not programmed to sin. Neither is God the author of evil. Each person is tempted by one's own desires (Jas. 1:13–15).

Christ's remedy for this fallen world is not to destroy human freedom, but to provide human freedom with the opportunity to pursue a more exquisite good: to become as perfect as our Heavenly Father is perfect. This means that every person must change. "I appeal to you therefore, brethren, by the mercies of God, to present your bodies as a living sacrifice, holy and acceptable to God, which is your spiritual worship. Do not be conformed to this world but be transformed by the renewal of your mind, that you may prove what is the will of God, what is good, acceptable, and perfect" (Ro. 12:1–2). Such change is painful and costly and places upon each person's shoulder one's own unique cross. For whoever refuses to bear one's cross cannot call oneself a disciple of Christ (Lk. 14:27).

We are human beings created in the image of God, with a moral integrity grounded in our free will given us by our Creator. Therefore, we must choose whom we shall serve. "No one can serve two masters; for either he will hate the one and love the other, or he will be devoted to the one and despise the other. You cannot serve God and mammon" (Mt. 6:24). We are all called to perfection, to become like Christ who is in the form (*morphe*) of God. And although it may be difficult—especially when one's sinful tendencies have become habits or even hardened into addictions—nevertheless: "No temptation has overtaken you that is not common to man. God is faithful and he will not let you be tempted beyond your strength, but with the temptation will also provide the way of escape, that you may be able to endure it" (1 Cor. 10:23). Therefore, the prayer that we are not brought to the test is also a plea for the grace of perseverance which has always been the lament of the *anawim*, the people of God. "Blessed are they who mourn, for they shall be comforted."

But deliver us from evil. This final petition, the seventh, completes the previous one with its expression of the hope that we shall most certainly be delivered from all evil. Christianity has no notion of an eternal struggle between equal evil principles as was the case with paganism. The God of the Judaeo-Christian tradition is the Creator of all that exists and, therefore, has no opposing equal power. Nothing can stand before his awesome majesty.

In this petition the Greek word *poneros* is generally translated as evil, since the article *ho* "the" is missing, and there is no evidence that Hebrew or Aramaic ever referred to Satan as the evil one. Also *The Didache* (see Appendix), which contains an identical Lord's Prayer, goes on to expand upon this prayer saying in 10:5: "Remember, Lord, thy Church, to deliver her from all evil." Nevertheless, evil is such an obvious and malicious fact of existence to the extent that many philosophers have considered it to be a real force. Of course, it has always been the teaching of the Church in accordance with what it has received from the Lord, that evil has behind it an active and malevolent intelligence. Hence, by extension it is proper to understand that the evil one is also implicated by Jesus in this petition to be delivered from (all) evil.

After all, evil is only a lack or distortion of what is good. By itself evil is purely contingent upon the good which it corrupts: it therefore demands an explanatory principle. While some evils in society can be accounted for by cultural or psychological conditioning, it is not enough when considering the prevalence of moral evil to try to explain it in terms of those factors alone. Only an intrusive evil principle is capable of distorting and corrupting the good which is inherent in all that God has created. Because nature is sustained by a holy and benevolent providence, it cannot admit of evil unless a freely acting evil principle interjects. Something else has to ignite the fuse.

Nor does it suffice to place the problem of evil *solely* within the free will of humans—who incidentally have also been created as basically good—since it is our constant tragedy that we often find our best intentions confronted by what is patently organized evil. It is not unusual to observe, that as soon as one undertakes something noble, virtuous, or holy, all hell breaks loose. Thus, individual free will is insufficient to encompass the all-inclusive and prevalent dominion of methodically directed evil, which betrays such an ominous aspect in our time.

Our Lord's instruction to pray to be delivered from evil is, therefore, a grave and ever urgent supplication. It includes far more than praying for the reforming of faulty or oppressive institutions, or the correction of erroneous thoughts and disordered passions, however desirable and necessary that may be. It also includes the prayer for the final casting out of that malevolence whom the Lord has declared "is a liar and the father of lies" and who has been "a murderer from the beginning" (Jn. 8:44).

For evil will finally be expunged. Of that we have Christ's sure promise. There can be no peace on earth until the final dénouement when Our Lord returns in triumph. The prayer for the deliverance from evil is, therefore, also a prayer for the eventual consummation of that promised kingdom of peace. "Blessed are the peacemakers: they shall be called sons of God."

> [16] When you are fasting, do not put on a gloomy look as the hypocrites do: they go about looking unsightly to let people know they are fasting. In truth I tell you, they have had their reward. [17] But when you fast, put scent on your head and wash your face, [18] so that no one will know you are fasting except your Father who sees all that is done in secret; and your Father who sees all that is done in secret will reward you.

From alms giving and prayer, Jesus now moves to address the third pillar of piety: fasting. Fasting was well known to the Jews of that time and included more than refraining from certain foods on various holy days. This self-denial comprised abstaining from eating, drinking, marital intimacy, washing, anointing, or even wearing sandals.[11] Fasting was required on the Day of Atonement as well as

---

11. Charles Quarles, *Sermon on the Mount*, p. 224.

the Jewish New Year; and there was also fasting at times of national crisis and personal tragedy. Over time such fasts began to multiply, e.g.: from sunrise to sunset; for periods of seven days, three weeks, or forty days.[12] And, of course we also note, in both Luke 18:12 and *Didache* 8:1, the custom of the Pharisees—and the early Christians—to fast twice a week.

Our Lord also fasted during his testing in the desert before he chose his disciples. However, it seems this was not typical of his disciples under him. When the disciples of John the Baptist challenged Jesus about this he replied: "Can the wedding guests mourn when the bridegroom is with them? But the time will come when the bridegroom is taken away from them, and then they will fast" (Mt. 9:14–16). Fasting was generally connected with mourning, but there was no need for mourning while the disciples had Jesus with them. Rather, this was to be a time for rejoicing.

As with alms and prayer so also with fasting Jesus again warns us of hypocrisy. Such warnings are present in the Old Testament as well (cf. Is. 58:1–12; Jer. 36:9, 23–25; Joel 2:12–17). But Jesus points out the danger of hypocrisy in this, namely, that it was done for the purpose of receiving the reward of admiration by others. In this instance as in the previous two, Jesus repeats the phrase: "In truth I tell you, they have had their reward" since their motive was not to make an authentic offering to God, and thus they violated the integrity of that spiritual communion. Rather, fasting like the other two acts of piety should reflect the intimate exchange between God and the devout person. It is within that secret place where the soul is substantially present with God that the "Father who sees all that is done in secret will reward you."

The self-denial that is involved all forms of fasting or asceticism is one of the most universally recognized ways of entering into unity with God, the soul's ultimate reward. All religions have taught it and all the saints have practised it; for its formative principle is to withdraw the soul's affections away from the world and the flesh, in order that she may be free to contemplate the presence of God. The purpose of all fasting is purification, i.e., the removal of impurities

12. Jg. 20:26; 2 Sam. 1:12; 3:35; 1 Sam. 31:13; Dan. 10:3; Ex. 34:2, 28; Dt. 9:9, 18.

from body and soul. Such is what Jesus intends when he speaks of anointing the head and washing the face.

The anointing of the head is a metaphor for the consecration of the intellect with the wisdom to serve God. In the Old Testament anointing of the head was done in order to consecrate a person for a divine office (Ex. 40:13; 1 Sam. 16:3, 13; 1 Kgs. 19:16). It inaugurated the crowning of that person with the wisdom and virtue necessary to fulfil the solemn tasks to be undertaken by the individual.

However, in the New Testament anointing refers to the reception by the disciple of that same Holy Spirit which rested upon Jesus like a dove when he received the waters of baptism (Lk. 3:21; 4:18). This anointing by the Holy Spirit is a confirmation that the disciple is in Christ Jesus: "it is God who gives us, with you, a sure place in Christ and has both anointed us and marked us with his seal, giving us as pledge the Spirit in our hearts" (2 Cor. 1:21). Immediately after his anointing, Jesus withdrew into the wilderness where he fasted for forty days, having been led there by the Holy Spirit (Lk. 4:1). Similarly, when we undertake any form of fasting, we ought also to submit to the direction of the Holy Spirit who will likewise lead us into that deserted place where we can sojourn with Our Lord where he dwells.

The act of washing the face is evocative of the purification of the heart directed to God, since it is the pure in heart who will see God face to face. Again, just as Jesus received the Spirit at his baptism, so his encouragement to wash our faces should recall to us our baptism also. It is the nature of baptism that it has washed away the guilt of original sin, marked our rebirth into the kingdom of God, united us with Christ, and has given us the gifts of the Holy Spirit. Immediately upon our baptism we were entirely purified. Therefore, when we undergo a fast Our Lord has urged us also to wash our faces, i.e., to cleanse ourselves of all that is duplicitous or unseemly, so that the heart is single and sincere and that our sacrifice may be acceptable to God.

With the two faculties of mind and heart, intellect and will, ordered to God he will then reward the soul in secret. How could it be otherwise? For should we make our minds receptive to his Spirit, having purified our hearts from all that would disturb us, "our house being stilled," we shall have come back to the deeper mansions of the soul only to discover his everlasting presence there, pouring grace into our hearts.

> ¹⁹ Do not store up treasures for yourselves on earth, where moth and woodworm destroy them and thieves can break in and steal. ²⁰ But store up treasures for yourselves in Heaven, where neither moth nor woodworm destroys them and thieves cannot break in and steal. ²¹ For wherever your treasure is, there will your heart be too. ²² The lamp of the body is the eye. It follows that if your eye is clear, your whole body will be filled with light. ²³ But if your eye is diseased, your whole body will be darkness. If then, the light inside you is darkened, what darkness that will be! ²⁴ No one can be the slave of two masters: he will either hate the first and love the second, or be attached to the first and despise the second. You cannot be the slave both of God and of mammon.

All our acts of piety must be done with pure intention. We should not practise the pious acts of alms, prayer, and fasting for the sake of worldly rewards, but rather, they must be offered solely to Our Heavenly Father. Our real treasure is in Heaven, not in this passing world.

The things of this world are transient and finite: our clothing and fabrics are prey to moths, our utensils and furniture susceptible to rust and woodworm (the Greek word *brosis* means eaten up), and our money and possessions are vulnerable to thieves.

> The covetous man is never satisfied with money, and the lover of wealth reaps no fruit from it; so this too is vanity. Where goods increase, parasites abound. Of what advantage are they to the owner except to feast his eyes upon? (Eccl. 5:9)

This world with all it contains is utterly contingent and limited in all its aspects. The perfections of a stone are not the perfections of a flower; neither are the attributes of a lion the attributes of the lamb. Rivers and lakes, mountains and valleys all have their grandeur and perils, but they do not last: time can change any one of them into the other. The stars and galaxies coalesce, grow, and violently die. And one way or another, this splendid universe itself will come to an end. Ultimately, all the treasures we shall have laid up on earth will perish.

Remember your Creator in the days of your youth,
   before the evil days come,
And the years approach when you will say,
   I have no pleasure in them;
Before the sun and the light, and the moon,
   and the stars, are darkened,
   before the clouds return after the rain;
In the day when the keepers of the house tremble,
   and the strong men are bent,
And the grinders cease because they are few,
And they who gaze out of the windows are blind.

...

Before the silver cord is snapped asunder
   and the golden bowl is broken,
And the pitcher is shattered at the spring,
   and the broken pulley falls into the well,
And the dust returns to the earth as it once was,
And the spirit returns to God who gave it.
Vanity of vanities, says the Preacher, all is vanity.
                      (Eccl. 12:1–3; 6–8)

Therefore, it behoves us to seek the things that last and which are of inherent worth. Such are the things of Heaven, which are eternal, spiritual, holy, and unfathomable. They are in essence the true treasure for which we were created and destined. For our human spirit is never satisfied with what is incomplete and temporal.

In the first place, our animal nature with its desires and tendencies is easily satiated. Eventually our nervous system becomes desensitized to sensory stimuli. Consequently, more and more nervous stimulation is required to generate the endorphins in the pleasure-producing centres in our brains. Under certain circumstances this can lead to addictions or even compulsions when our behavior has become disordered. How often do we witness compulsions for shopping, gambling, or perpetual youth; or addictions to alcohol, pornography, or unnatural acts? For such desires have no natural object; neither are they subordinated to reason. Because we, unlike other animals, lack the instincts which restrict or organize these passions, they spiral beyond rational control. They then imprison us, degrade us, and eventually restrain our free-will, compelling us to behave less than human, and to fall even lower than the beasts (Ps. 49:12, 20; Ro. 1:26–32). They can never satisfy: for "this is vanity and a chasing after wind."

In the second place, our spiritual nature can never receive into itself the material substances of this world as such. We do not receive into our minds a mountain, lightening, or a black hole, but rather their abstracted forms. However, these objects, because they contain the ideas of their Creator, always point beyond themselves to the One who created them and made them intelligible. They are insufficient to explain themselves. Therefore, numbers lead us to seek the formal unity behind them; material processes demand an initial efficient cause; the brevity of life leads to thoughts of immortality; and moral behavior requires that its formal good is found. But these are just so many separated things which themselves require something further that unifies them all. Reason requires truth; our aesthetic sense seeks the beautiful, and intuition strives to lose itself in the sublime.

Nothing is complete in and of itself, and our spirit, sensing this profoundly, is not fulfilled until it is united with the highest good. This is especially so, for we desire nothing that does not contain some good. Yet all created things being limited always point beyond themselves, and as a consequence the heart transported ever upwards has no rest. "This also is vanity and a chasing after wind." Only that good which is eternal and unlimited can ever satisfy the desire of the soul for the infinite good.

And that infinite good is God: "For with thee is the fountain of life; and in thy light we shall see light" (Ps. 36:9). Just as the lamp lights up the entire room, so when the eye of the soul is filled with the light of God then one's whole person is illuminated. However, if we turn away from God to these vain things passing before us, then the eyes of our souls will "become diseased" or disordered (*poneros* can mean diseased, degenerate, or evil). Having turned from the light to what is unseemly, our souls will become darkened; and it will be the darkness of anxiety and of despair, since what we have taken for our security has become the source of our insecurity. "Vanity of vanities, says the Preacher, all is vanity."

Therefore, we must find our treasure in Heaven since we cannot serve two masters. We have witnessed how the things of this world can enslave us, since where our treasure is there is our heart also. If we allow these vain things to attain mastery over us, they will then determine what we will value and what we will despise. The human spirit is such that it is impossible to love two contraries which compete for our devotion. But the things of this world have a nature opposite to the things of Heaven. The former are finite, temporal, imperfect, shallow, material, and ephemeral. The latter is infinite, eternal, perfect, profound, spiritual, and holy.

The things of this world become mammon when they become objects of devotion: i.e., when they become idols. The word "mammon" has the same Aramaic root as "amen" which means "truly" or "verily." But the prefix *mu*, "for," gives to "mammon" the meaning of: something towards which one is inordinately devoted. In other words mammon refers to anything made into a fetish, i.e., riches, privileges, fame, power. There is an instructive play on this meaning in Luke 16:11: "If therefore you have not been *faithful* in the unrighteous *mammon*, who will *entrust to you* the *true* riches?" That is, if one has not behaved trustworthily towards the tainted riches of this world, how can one be trusted to deal appropriately with Heavenly things?

Again it is clear that Our Lord presupposes that we possess the free-will to choose whom or what we shall serve. Our Lord has given us the choice of serving him in his righteous kingdom or becoming slaves of this world. We can either be slaves to mammon or slaves to Christ.

> For when you were slaves of sin, you were free from righteousness. But what fruit did you get then from the things of which you are now ashamed? For the end of those things is death. But now that you have been freed from sin and have become slaves of God, the fruit that you have leads to sanctification, and its end is eternal life. For the wages of sin is death, but the gift of God is eternal life in Christ Jesus our Lord. (Ro. 6:20–23)

St. Francis once said in his "Admonitions" that "all the creatures under heaven, each according to its nature, serve, know, and obey their Creator better than you." Both the inorganic world and the organic obey the laws of the Creator far better than we do. Yet God cares for us much more than he does for them. Thus although we are to relinquish our concern for worldly goods, this is no cause for anxiety. We are God's creatures after all...

> [25] That is why I am telling you not to worry about your life and what you are to eat, nor about your body and what you are to wear. Surely life is more than food, and the body more than clothing! [26] Look at the birds in the sky. They do not sow or reap or gather into barns; yet your Heavenly Father feeds them. Are you not worth much more than they are? [27] Can any of you, however much you worry, add one single cubit to your span of life? [28] And why worry about clothing? Think of the flowers growing in the fields; they never have to work or spin; [29] yet I assure you that not even Solomon in all his royal robes was clothed like one of these. [30] Now if that is how God clothes the wild flowers growing in the field which are there today and thrown into the furnace tomorrow, will he not much more look after you, you who have so little faith? [31] So do not worry; do not say, "What are we to eat? What are we to drink? What are we to wear?" [32] It is the gentiles who set their hearts on all these things. Your Heavenly Father knows you need them all. [33] Set your hearts on his kingdom first, and on God's saving justice, and all these other things will be given you as well. [34] So do not worry about tomorrow: tomorrow will take care of itself. Each day has enough trouble of its own.

Do we really know our essential worth—not in our own eyes, but absolutely before God? Do we appreciate what it actually means to be made in the image and likeness of God (Gen. 1:26–27)? Because of this divine likeness we possess a profound dignity. Such nobility could not have ever come from the pursuance of worldly things which can never satisfy, for they are limited and we are created for the infinite. Neither the human body nor the soul can ever be satisfied with what is incomplete. Moreover, we have seen how these things can enslave and degrade us. Even so, our spirit strives to transcend the finite and to strain towards perfection.

Ancient and classical thought has recognized that there are four distinctive qualities that transcend all attempts to put them into categories, but which are also intimated in all that exists. They are unity, truth, goodness, and beauty. Every concrete thing that the mind can identify has these qualities to a lesser or greater perfection. Every conceivable thing has the unity of its own identity in which it is recognizable as a complete whole: as this nameable thing present before us, immediately graspable by the mind. Each identifiable object has the constancy of its form by which it remains the intelligible thing that it is. All creatures receive the goodness or perfection of their natures given them by the Creator. And all disclose their internal harmony, splendor, and integrity. Our minds have the ability to contemplate and appreciate these things, which raise us far above the natural world which can never sense such things. By this ability our natural dignity is manifested.

These transcendentals are also the source of all the human arts. We seek unity in mathematics, metaphysics and the natural sciences; and we investigate truth in logic and rhetoric. In ethics and in social and political thought we try to discover and establish what is good and just; and in art, music, and literature we strain to express the beautiful. All of us possess the nobility to reflect on these things to some degree. Qualities such as these even inspire us in those rarer moments to those sublime intimations that only poets can express:

> When I behold the heavens, the work of your fingers,
> The moon and the stars which you have established—
> What is man that you should be mindful of him,
> Or the son of man that you should care for him?
>
> Yet you have made him a little less than the angels,
> You have crowned him with glory and honour,
> Given him dominion of the works of your hands,
> And put all things under his feet.

The very fact that in reading those words you can follow and be moved by them betrays your spiritual dignity. It is the nobility of your human spirit that you have this capacity to transcend the finitude of the mundane and soar to the sublimity of heavenly contemplation. Yet this intuitive sense comes from something very simple and humble. In the summit of one's soul, there is a point where God touches the soul communicating to her beauty and form, infusing the spark (*scintilla*) of life and goodness. This mental *habitus* or faculty flows from God's Truth into his image. And, though it is infinitely distinct from the nature of God, yet it is intimately embraced in his substance.

We, who are made in the image of God have the ability to reflect upon the nature of things. It is this simple capacity to think about being that puts us in touch with those transcendent attributes which all things possess. God ceaselessly imparts intelligible form to all creatures according to their limits. Our souls possess the capacity to contemplate in each thing those created forms or ideas. But our awareness of our own being, that soul's intuition of her own existence, is just that sense of God speaking to us at the highest point of our souls.

> The human reason—or rather, the human soul in so far as it is rational—is truly the temple of almighty God, where he is chiefly fain to dwell . . . it has an apex, the highest point in the spiritual faculty of reason. No light of human reasoning functions there; the mind simply knows, the will simply acts, forcing the soul to acknowledge and submit to the truth of God, and to his will. For although faith, hope and charity lavish their heavenly impulses on practically all the soul's faculties, reasonable as well as sensitive, although they bring those faculties to submit to the rightful authority of the theological virtues—yet their special domain, where clearly those virtues naturally belong, is the soul's highest point.[13]

This is the scintilla, that spark which is kept unstained by God, where he tenderly speaks your name calling each of you unto himself.

All human beings are touched in this way. Indeed, from the first moment of conception a spiritual form comes to the human body which is already of a nature predisposed to receive it; so that the *communication* of this vital spark of life (*psyche*), transmitted to that tiny body in the womb, acts as the template, as it were, in which this nascent life takes form. Thus there is never a moment when we are not cradled in the sustaining presence of God. Ultimately this is what constitutes our intrinsic dignity and worth.

Furthermore, our baptism has restored to our fallen human nature the dignity it lost through the fall making us the adopted

---

13. St. Francis de Sales, *The Love of God,* pp. 26–27.

children of the Father. Our baptism in Christ Jesus has placed us in his kingdom where he reigns communicating grace into our souls through his Holy Spirit. We receive the gifts of the Holy Spirit, the theological virtues are infused into us, and we are heirs to everlasting life. We are temples of the Blessed Trinity!

Even more, we receive from the Most Holy Trinity the grace of justification which enables us, through the infused virtues, to believe in God (*CCC* 1266). It is the nature of this unmerited gift of faith that it reconnects us at our deepest centre with God. Faith has a unitive function by virtue of our consenting will, which orients us to God and receives from him sanctifying grace. This is so since, because faith is a supernatural gift, it establishes the believer in a certain conviction, simply because it places its trust in the One revealing: Christ Jesus Our Lord.

As a result our souls are constituted as a supernatural organism. The soul is the subject in which this organism is formed. Grace is the formative principle of this mystical body, elevating us and constituting us in the supernatural life. It makes us just and pleasing to God, giving us the capacity for receiving condign and congruent merit. Above all it enables us to love God, to hope and to trust in him, and to dwell ever more intimately with him. "For I am certain of this: neither death nor life, nor angels, nor principalities, nothing already in existence and nothing still to come, nor any power, nor the heights nor the depths, nor any created thing whatever, will be able to come between us and the love of god, known to us in Christ Jesus our Lord" (Ro. 8:39).

"That is why I am telling you not to worry about your life and what you are to eat, nor about your body and what you are to wear." It is because you are worth much more than the birds and the flowers that you need not be anxious about these things. "Your Heavenly Father knows you have need of them." The description of God as "your Heavenly Father" indicates that you who truly follow Jesus—you who primarily seek the kingdom of God and his righteousness—are especially dear to him. You are among those whom Our Lord has called Blessed; and all these things shall be yours as well. Our Lord is not forbidding the disciple to do whatever is needful for satisfying the wants of life. Jesus only exhorts us not to be over-solicitous and anxious. He is concerned that his disciples do not become disquieted by a longing for what they do not have or be unduly worried about what is beyond their control, with the result that his disciples would deprive themselves of the peace and tranquillity of those (*anawim*) who do trust in him.

The New Covenant does not exist outside God's providence. Our faith has placed us in the kingdom of God where, much more than any secular ruler, he will look after his wayfaring subjects: "you who have so little faith," or more literally "little faiths" (*oligopistoi*). We are so blind: "For some of us believe that God is almighty and may do all; and that he is all-wisdom and can do all; but that he is all-love, and will do all—there we fail."[14] We fail because our loyalties are split; we still keep one eye on the vanities of this world. Our anxieties arise because we have placed our trust in things which are fleeting, corruptible, or can be taken from us. One cannot serve two masters; hence we are encouraged to seek the kingdom first, lest we become enslaved by those passing things which the pagans seek. Do they not see that the mammon they have made to be their security has become the very source of their insecurity?

But which of us by taking thought could add one cubit to our span of life "since man's days are measured out, and the number of his months depends on Thee, and since Thou hast fixed the limit he cannot pass" (Job 14:5)? There is a time to live and a time to die, but both of these are in God's hands. It is enough that we concern ourselves with what we can look after today. Therefore, trust in God, place yourselves in his presence and be not anxious for those things beyond your immediate horizon. For the disciple who lives in the present moment, in the presence of God, it is always today; and the morrow, whose approach had been feared, will have taken care of itself.

But if the kingdom of God, and the righteousness which is its ethos, is our primary desire then we will discover that everything else will be subordinated and properly ordered to it. "Blessed are those who hunger and thirst for righteousness, for they shall be filled." Our yearning for the righteousness of the kingdom arises

14. Julian of Norwich, *The Revelations of Divine Love*, cp. 73.

from the acknowledgement of our moral and spiritual poverty—
our need for Christ "our righteousness, holiness and redemption"
(1 Cor. 1:30). Yet the poor in spirit are blessed for "theirs is the kingdom of heaven." By setting our hearts on Christ and his kingdom
before all else, we shall have impoverished our spirits of worldly
vanities; but we shall have secured for ourselves a substantial dwelling that no storm can topple. Then we shall have peace and shall
communicate our peace, and we "shall be called children of God."
The Father will clothe us with the virtues of mercy and meekness.
We shall "have the earth for our inheritance," and our mourning
will have turned to joy. Our eye will be single, our hearts pure, and
we shall dwell among the Blessed who shall see God. The kingdom
of Heaven will be ours. "For the kingdom of God is not eating and
drinking; but righteousness, and peace, and joy in the Holy Spirit"
(Ro. 14:17).

6

The Lord, Our God

THE KINGDOM OF GOD is the reign of Christ in our hearts; the principles and precepts which separate us from the sway of the world, the flesh and the devil; as well as the Church founded upon his apostles; and the kingdom yet to come. Thus, the kingdom is everything that falls under the Christ, pertains to him, and proceeds from him. It is the whole Christ in all his majesty and movement. It is the presence of Christ himself; for he brings the kingdom, since all authority in Heaven and earth has been given to him. Our Blessed Lord's sermon has brought us squarely into the kingdom of Heaven. But, lest we—like Lot's wife—hesitate to look back upon Sodom with nostalgic eyes, we are given a number of codicils that will help to keep us securely in the kingdom of God.

7 ¹Do not judge, and you will not be judged; ²because the judgements you give are the judgements you will get, and the standard you use will be the standard used for you. ³Why do you observe the splinter in your brother's eye and never notice the great log in your own? ⁴And how dare you say to your brother, "Let me take that splinter out of your eye," when, look, there is a great log in your own? ⁵Hypocrite! Take the log out of your own eye first, and then you will see clearly enough to take the splinter out of your brother's eye. ⁶Do not give dogs what is holy; and do not throw your pearls in front of pigs, or they may trample them and then turn on you and tear you to pieces.

By now it should have been clear to Jesus' listeners that to seek the kingdom is to seek its righteousness, which must be done in faith and with a pure intention. However, there are many ways the people of God can spoil this simple-hearted spirit. One of these is our tendency to self-righteousness which can manifest itself in both spiritual blindness to ourselves and a judgemental attitude towards others. This attitude was illustrated in Our Lord's parable of the Pharisee and the tax collector, whose meaning can also be taken as a metaphor for the perennial blindness of Israel as revealed in Kings and Chronicles, and as the basis for Jesus' diatribes against the hypocrisy of the scribes and the Pharisees. This is a particularly virulent disease which can infect one's soul and rob one's spiritual life of all sincerity. It has been the source of division, recrimination, and conflict between Christians. In short, it can corrupt true religion itself.

Yet on the other hand are we not required to form judicious opinions regarding the behavior of our neighbour? Are we to sit back indifferently when we notice some evil or error being promoted or enacted before us, especially when it is apparent that such errors can have malevolent repercussions on the community? Surely the gospel of loving our neighbour requires that we give help and correction when one is in moral or spiritual peril? After all, it is a question of eternal life. However, the last two verses of this portion of the sermon should make it clear that turning a blind eye is not the demanded response. One can form just judgements provided one's own eye or conscience is clear. Furthermore, this is essential if we are to ensure we do not cast our pearls before swine or give what is holy to dogs.

In order to elucidate Our Lord's meaning here it will be helpful if we turn to consider Luke's rendition of this same passage:

> Be compassionate just as your Father is compassionate. Do not judge, and you will not be judged; do not condemn, and you will not be condemned; forgive, and you will be forgiven. Give, and it will be given to you: good measure, pressed down, shaken together, and overflowing, will be poured into your lap; because the measure you use will be the measure you get back. (Vs. 6:38)

Then follows the parable about the blind leading the blind, with the consequence that both fall into the ditch!

What Our Lord is requiring, then, is authenticity and mercy when dealing with the errors and waywardness of others. To discriminate justly is morally necessary; to be hypercritical, especially when one's own guilt is far worse—symbolized by the hyperbole of the beam in one's eye—is reprehensible. Moreover, if one is in error then one can only lead the other astray, like the blind leading the blind. "Hypocrite! Take the log out of your own eye first, and then you will see clearly enough to take the splinter out of your brother's eye."

One is reminded of the spiritual condition of King David when he condemned "without mercy" a rich man who, as the prophet Nathan had alleged in a parable, had stolen and killed a poor man's ewe lamb. The King's judgement was that the rich man was to be put to death and that a four-fold restitution was to be made to the poor man for his ewe. David did not see that in condemning the rich man he was passing sentence on himself. For David had taken Uriah the Hittite's wife, Bathsheba, for his own after having put him to the sword (1 Sam. 12:1–10). The judgement that was to be meted out to David (before his repentance) was at least equal to that which he had apportioned to the rich man. Since King David had judged without mercy and since he was not in a state of grace because of his grave sins, then divine justice had to be apportioned to him in turn. Here we see a divine principle in action: to those who show mercy, mercy will be given; but those who refuse mercy will find themselves before God's judgement. David had reaped what he sowed, because he had chosen to place himself under God's justice instead of his mercy. "Blessed are the merciful: for they shall obtain mercy." "Condemn not, and you will not be condemned."

This story of King David and Nathan the prophet offers even further instruction: for we can only imagine what would have happened if Nathan had been treated like the prophet Amos, from the land of Tekoa, who was tortured and slain by a priest of Bethel; or Obadiah who endured much evil from King Ahab. The prophet Habbakuk was stoned by the Jews in Jerusalem, as was Jeremiah the son of Hilkiah who was also thrown and abandoned into a cistern. Joash the king slew the prophet Zechariah, the son of Berachiah, between the steps and the altar, and sprinkled his blood upon the horns of the altar.[1] Fortunately for Nathan, King David was unlike

---

1. Earnest A. Wallis Budge, ed., *The Book of the Bee* (Oxford: the Clarendon Press, 1886), ch. XXXII.

any of these, since he respected the office of the prophet and was open to his correction.

All these historical details emphasize a number of the points that Jesus is making in this passage. First, Jesus twice depicts the judgement as being directed toward "your" brother, i.e., one's fellow Christian. This is what the prophet Nathan did, since he was concerned for the soul of David, the King of Israel, and his future (Messianic) kingdom. Similarly, our correction of our brethren in Christ must be done for wholesome motives of genuine concern for the brethren's spiritual and moral welfare. Secondly, Nathan spoke tactfully to David in the form of a parable and was merciful to him when David repented. Thirdly, Nathan was sent by God and was guiltless when he accused David. King David was the guilty one who, as it were, had the beam in his eye; while Nathan's eye was clear. Finally, Nathan knew that he would not be casting his pearls before swine nor giving holy things to dogs, since King David was God's own anointed.

Both wild dogs and swine were unclean things (*debarim tame'im*) in Judaism (Ex. 22:30; Lev. 11:7; Pr. 26:11); and Jews were forbidden to eat them, or touch their carcasses, or even keep them in their homes. Because these animals represented what was contemptible, they were often used as derogatory epithets (1 Sam. 17:43; 24:15; 2 Sam. 9:8; 16:9; Is. 66:3, 17). Indeed, Revelation 22:15 associates dogs with fortune tellers, fornicators (*pornoi*), murderers, idolaters, and liars. There is also an interesting usage in *Didache* 9: "No one is to eat or drink of your Eucharist but those who have been baptized in the name of the Lord; for the Lord's own saying applies here, 'Do not give that which is holy unto dogs.'" Clearly, as this verse states, the Eucharist is one of those holy things to which "the Lord's own saying applies." But it is only one example. And because the context of the sermon's passage is about judgement, then we must not limit Our Lord's word to the Eucharist only, although the Blessed Sacrament is most certainly to be treated as sacred just as the *Didache* intends.

Also, no distinction needs to be made between pearls given to swine and holy things given to dogs, for these phrases are just an application of the rhetorical device of repetition in Hebrew poetry and teaching. For example in Zech. 9:9 we have a beautiful instance of two repetitions, one at the beginning and at the end:

> Rejoice greatly, O daughter of Zion;
> shout, O daughter of Jerusalem:
> behold, thy King cometh unto thee:
> he is just, and having salvation;
> lowly, and riding upon an ass,
> and upon a colt the foal of an ass.

Another example can be given from Ps. 30:8: "I cried to thee, Lord; and unto the Lord I made supplication." Many other examples could be given.[2] This device was used for emphasis or for amplification of the initial idea. The latter was also Jesus' intention: i.e., do not give what are pearls/holy things to swine/dogs because they will scorn them and then turn on you. It is apparent that Jesus himself has united the two admonitions in the concluding phrase to this passage.

Combining all the preceding it should be clear that Jesus is teaching us that whatever is set apart for God, and as a result is holy, should be treated with due reverence and not entrusted to those who are manifestly hostile or hardened in their wickedness. Even Jesus admonished his disciples not to go into the regions of Samaria or into any gentile town. They were required to preach first to the lost sheep of Israel. Yet if they should not be welcomed in any town or the people refused to listen, the disciples were instructed to "kick the dust off their feet" as they left: the judgement upon that town would be worse than that inflicted upon Sodom and Gomorrah (Mt. 10:5, 12–15).

Jesus himself illustrates his own use of tact in the case of the Canaanite woman whose daughter was tormented by a devil (Mt. 15:21–28). Her persistence was at first ignored by Jesus even after his disciples pleaded with him to give her what she wanted, since she was making a nuisance of herself. Jesus' reply was consistent with his earlier instructions to his disciples that he came only to the lost sheep of the House of Israel. However, the woman approached Jesus,

2. Gen. 4:23–24; Num. 23:21, 23; 24:17; Ps.31:2; 50:20; 63:6; 72:1–2; Is. 60: 1–3; Jer. 12:1; Ez. 21:19; Mic. 3:10; 4:1–2.

paid him obeisance by bowing low before him, and begged him to help her. Then, testing her, Jesus said: "It is not fair to take the children's bread and throw it to the dogs." But when she reposted that "even the dogs eat the crumbs that fall from their master's (*kyrion*) table," he remarked: "Great is your faith! Be it done as you desire." And her daughter was healed. Much more than the woman's persistence, her humility, wisdom, and even obeisance before Jesus, it was her faith which was praised and which merited for her the healing she desired. This was a gracious gift that Jesus had wanted to give her (over and above the healing of her daughter): the approbation and affirmation of her faith.

It should be clear by now what the meaning of "judgement" is. It is most certainly not the kind of judgement first made by King David which was given without mercy and from a duplicitous and condemnatory attitude. This leads nowhere except to harden the heart of the one giving the condemnation and the alienation of the one being judged. The proper use of judgement is from a clear and honest heart given in a loving and generous spirit. This gives the other person the context in which to respond favorably and receptively. The former is destructive to everyone concerned; while the latter enhances even the one giving correction. "Brethren, if anyone among you errs from the truth, and another brings him back to it, you should know that anyone who converts a sinner from the error of his way will be saving a soul from death and covering over a multitude of sins" (Jm. 5:19–20).

Therefore, there is no contradiction between exercising discretion and what Jesus had said earlier in the sermon about letting one's light shine before others. In fact, giving correction is one example of doing just that. The Lord simply makes clear how this is to be done. Neither is there a contradiction with his earlier admonition of our being prepared for the prospect of suffering persecution when we witness to the Gospel. In warning us to be wary of being trampled and torn to pieces by swine and dogs, Jesus is not forbidding us from risking persecution on his account. Rather, he is saying that one should use one's discretion when one preaches the Gospel or upbraids unrighteousness. If this is done from genuine motives of mercy and of giving glory to our Father in Heaven, then

if you should be persecuted "in the cause of uprightness: the kingdom of Heaven is yours.... Rejoice and be glad, for your reward
will be great in heaven; this is how they persecuted the prophets
before you."

There is another application of this passage, and that is to us. Often
we judge ourselves too harshly and find it difficult to feel we are forgiven or even to forgive ourselves. It may be the case that the penitent soul has understood something of the mercy and goodness of
the Lord; such that the more one sees God's mercy towards oneself,
the greater the indignation and shame is felt for the contempt one's
sins have shown towards Him. Consequently, the penitent cannot
rest in God's forgiveness, but feels that one must offer some super-
erogatory atonement or humiliation for past offences committed
against so merciful, generous, and innocent a Saviour. Although the
more one is offered comfort and reassurance by well-meaning persons, yet—like pearls before swine—the greater one detests and
grieves for one's past failings and misdeeds. All that the penitent can
feel is dismay at one's past ingratitude to one's God, particularly to
One who has been so forgiving.

Such a person might discern whether this comes from a tendency
towards assuming that one ought to be above sinning, or if it comes
from a scrupulous zeal for uprightness. In either case, the mental
state is the same—and it is not always the vice of pride as one may
often hear. On the contrary, underlying this is remorse for the
spoiled nobility of one's soul, the dignity of which one senses; as
well as regret at never being able to repair the disordered effects of
one's own sins upon the divine economy. Both of these are natural
and genuine developments in the spiritual life. Both are manifesta-
tions of a burgeoning and profound love for the Lord; for we would
not have felt this way had we not loved so much. It is because we do
love God that we regret the thoughtless ways in which we have misused so much of what he has entrusted to us. This is the ultimate
source of our sorrow. There is no greater penance than constantly to
reflect upon the immensity of God's love for us and the constancy
of his faithfulness towards us; and yes, at the same time our own
unfaithfulness, ingratitude, and obstinacy towards our Beloved

Lord. We shall then find in all this that spark wherein we have loved our Lord all along, and that we have never really left his presence. "Blessed are you who mourn, for you shall be comforted."

> 7 Ask, and it will be given to you; search, and you will find; knock, and the door will be opened to you. 8 Everyone who asks receives; everyone who searches finds; everyone who knocks will have the door opened. 9 Is there anyone among you who would hand his son a stone when he asked for bread? 10 Or would hand him a snake when he asked for a fish? 11 If you, then, evil as you are, know how to give your children what is good, how much more will your Father in Heaven give good things to those who ask him! 12 So always treat others as you would like them to treat you; that is the Law and the Prophets.

We have been admonished not to judge others from a bad or faulty conscience; and we have been warned about the discretionary use of holy things. Both of these were given to ensure we do not disturb our peace in the kingdom. Now Jesus wants once again to reassure his people that they can trust that their Heavenly Father will give them the good things of the kingdom: all they have to do is ask, seek, and knock.

Jesus has already given us the structure and purpose of the ideal prayer. Prayer is not to be regarded as some magical incantation which treats God like some genie in a bottle who appears to do our bidding at our every whim. Rather we have been taught to pray for the coming of the kingdom and the fulfilment of God's will. We have been encouraged to pray for forgiveness, preservation from temptation, and deliverance from the evil one.

Also, Jesus has already reassured us that we need not worry about material needs, since our Heavenly Father who knows our needs can be trusted to provide for his servants their daily bread. Material rewards are the sort of thing with which the pagans are preoccupied. Furthermore, it should be clear from the beatitudes that the people of the kingdom (*anawim*) are desirous for more heavenly things. Jesus' disciples have a higher set of priorities: for they seek Heavenly treasure, not corruptible and transitory mammon. They thirst for holiness more than drink; and savor righteousness more than eating (Ro. 14:17).

This meaning is also supported by Luke's parallel passage (vs. 11:13) where the "good things" in Matthew have been replaced with the words "Holy Spirit." This also is Matthew's meaning, since in all other uses of the adjective *agathos* outside the sermon, he associates the term with virtue or personal goodness. In 7:17–18 the adjective is twice used to refer to the good fruit produced by a healthy tree, repeating a similar thought in 12:33–37. In verse 19:17 the word describes God who alone is good (*agathos*) in answer to the rich young ruler's *asking* about what good thing (*agathon*) he must do to *inherit eternal life*. The term is used again in 22:10 to contrast good people with evil ones and in 25:21, 23 for the "good and faithful servant." St. Matthew's consistent usage of the term "good things" for moral character, virtue, and good deeds fits well with those things produced by the Holy Spirit in St. Luke's understanding. Luke, in writing for a Greek readership, clarifies for gentiles Matthew's meaning of "good things" by specifying the gift of the Holy Spirit. (After all it was Luke alone who in Acts 1:6–8 described the descent of the Holy Spirit at Pentecost as the answer to their query about the restoration of the kingdom.) Matthew, on the other hand, is writing for a Jewish audience who knew the Psalms, wisdom literature, and rabbinic prayers and, therefore, already understood the sort of spiritual and moral gifts that ought to be prayed for.

This understanding that spiritual gifts are meant is also supported by the usage of the word "seek," for Jesus had already instructed us to "seek first the kingdom of God and his righteousness." Moreover, it is those who hunger and thirst for righteousness who will receive and who are described as Blessed. It is promised by the Lord that those who seek will find. The only other use of the term "find" in the sermon occurs in verse 14 where we shall see that only the few who genuinely seek the difficult road that leads to eternal life in the kingdom will be the ones who find it.

Finally, when we consider the usage of the word "knock" it is fairly obvious that it refers to entrance into the kingdom with the virtues it entails. For the following passage takes up the theme of entry into the narrow gate which leads to life everlasting, and it is upon such entrances that one knocks. In New Testament times gates to cities or to courtyards normally had within them a small entrance door upon which one knocked to gain entry from the gatekeeper. This is illustrated in Acts 12:13 where Simon Peter "knocked at the door (*thuran*) of the gateway" (*pulonos*) in the courtyard of the house of John Mark. The door within the gate served the convenient and secure purpose of admitting the occasional individual without having to open the entire gate, which would otherwise leave the walled city or house vulnerable to possible attack or entry by a larger group or mob. The door within the gate afforded the gatekeeper greater control over who entered the city or courtyard. It is those who knock on this portal who shall gain entry, since the door to the kingdom will be opened unto them.

Therefore, the context of the sermon, Luke's account, and the usage in the rest of Matthew support the interpretation that "ask, seek, and knock" refer to entrance into the kingdom and the gifts which the Holy Spirit will endow. Otherwise, we would be left to make the obvious objection from experience that God does not always give everything we ask for, even though Jesus had affirmed that he would.

But if it is spiritual gifts to which Jesus is referring here then the following metaphors make perfect sense: for what father would give his son a stone instead of bread or a serpent instead of a fish? There is a proportionality in these metaphors which is reflected in Jesus' continuation "how much more…" Bread differed from a stone not because of its appearance, since leavened bread in those days had the rounded shape of a stone not the rectangular shape to which we may be accustomed. Bread differs from a stone, then, because it belonged to a higher (organic) order. In contrast, a serpent differed from a fish because the former was among the unclean things that must not be eaten. Scaly fish were kosher, but sea serpents and their ersatz equivalent eels were among the forbidden foods. Both of these would have been ejected from the nets of fishermen in the Sea of Galilee, right below the mountain where Our Lord was speaking. Only fish with scales that could be removed were appropriate for human consumption. Like bread, fish also belonged to a higher order than serpents to the extent that they were also things that were beneficial for people. Both could be received internally and would provide sustenance and nutriments to the child.

Thus, in reflecting upon their respective proportionality, one may say that as bread is to stone and fish is to serpent—and father is to son—so God the Father is to his children in the good things he will give to them. What is more, as God is infinite in his transcendence so is he in his benevolence and mercy. Therefore, we may be secure in the confidence that when we ask, seek, and knock, Our Heavenly Father will be certain to give his children the good things of the kingdom: "There is no need to fear, little flock, for it has pleased the Father to give you the kingdom" (Lk. 12:32). Not the mammon of the pagans, of course, but "good measure, pressed down, shaken together, and overflowing, will be poured into your lap" (Lk. 6:38).

Of course, it is impossible for humans to behave with such infinite generosity towards others which the infinite Being of God can provide. And lest we feel daunted by this impossibility—and in order to preserve justice as well—Jesus summarizes and concludes this section with the *Golden Rule*: "So always treat others as you would like them to treat you; that is the Law and the Prophets." Jesus intends us to understand that this rule comprises the teaching given in both the Torah and the Prophetic writings; for it is found in Tobit 4:15, Sirach 31:15, and in the teaching attributed to Rabbi Hillel: "What is hateful to you, do not do to your neighbour; that is the whole Torah, while the rest is commentary thereon" (*Palestinian Targum, b. Shabbat* 31a).

It might be objected, however, that the positive form, in which Our Lord gives this rule, might also seem impossible to fulfil, for how can we do unto others literally "all things (*panta*) whatsoever you wish (*thelete*) that men should do to you"? If this phrase stood alone unconnected to the metaphor about the good things a father can give his children, then it would indeed seem impossible to fulfil the commandment to grant "all things whatsoever." However, it is not that all things whatsoever must be done, but what is proportionate within the reciprocal context of the situation. This requires one to extend towards others a sympathetic understanding of their needs by placing oneself in their position. Just as the father exercises empathy towards his son in recognizing and meeting his needs, so we must exercise the same understanding towards another person.

Thus the translation "treat others as you would like them to treat you" is closer to the intended meaning.

Furthermore, by pointing out that "this is the Law and the Prophets" Jesus indicates that the reciprocity contained in the Golden Rule must be understood and practised in the context of the covenant established between God the Father and his children made in his image, just as a son is the image of his father. The Law and the Prophets presuppose that covenant. So once again, the proper proportion between divine Justice and natural law is to be retained. Our interactions with others must be done *sub specie aeternitatis*. Taking all these things together the intended meaning is: one should act justly towards others in a given situation by giving others the dignity due to them, since they share the same dignity with you, because like you they are also made in the image of God. We must treat them as God's image, because, before God, that is how we should be treated. "Love your neighbour as like unto (*camocha*) yourself" (Lev. 19:18).

Now if all humankind is made in the image of God and if we are all one substance in the sense that we share with one another the same natural dignity created by God the Father, then how much more profoundly and intimately are we united with the brethren in whom dwell the Father, Son, and Holy Spirit? The life of the Holy Trinity is realized in the eternal generation of the Son from the Father, and by the procession of the Holy Spirit from the Father and the Son. Indeed, the life of the Holy Trinity is precisely that Spirit in which the Father begets the Son and the Son images the Father. In begetting the Son, the Father gives him everything that is his; and in receiving, the Son returns everything to the Father (Jn. 17:1–2; 4–5; 10; 22–23). The Son is the eternal utterance (*logos*) of the Father proceeding immediately from his substance, having the same form: a complete, well-defined image of God, fully and perfectly expressing his majesty, and divinity. Divine Wisdom lovingly and obediently proclaims and expresses the truth about the Father, for in the Godhead there is perfect concord. In the loving fecundity of the Spirit, the Father generates the Son so that the Son emanates from the Father, and in the Spirit of love the Son glorifies the Father. The breath (*ruach, pneuma*) of the Holy Trinity is immanent in the

Father, emanates with the Son, and returns back in the Holy Spirit. Thus, in the mysticism of St. John of the Cross, the Holy Spirit of love is the creative *ekstasis* of the Godhead.

In the beginning the Word was;
He lived in God
and possessed in him
his infinite happiness…

And thus the glory of the Son
was the Father's glory,
and the Father possessed
all his glory in the Son.
As the lover in the beloved
each lived in the other,
and the Love that unites them
is one with them…

In that immense love
proceeding from the two
the Father spoke words
of great affection to the Son,
words of such profound delight
that no one understood them…

"My Son, only your
company contents me,
and if something pleases me
I love that same thing in you…
I am pleased with you alone,
O life of my life!…"
"My Son, I wish to give you
a bride who will love you…"

"I am very grateful,"
the Son answered;
"I will show my brightness
to the bride you give me,
so that by it she may see
how great my Father is,
and how I have received
my being from your being."…

"Let it be done, then," said the Father,
"for your love has deserved it."
And by these words
the world was created,
a palace for the bride...

For as the Father and the Son
and he who proceeds from them
live in one another,
so it would be with the bride;
for, taken wholly into God,
she will live the life of God.

Romances 9:1–4

We who have been baptized in the name of the Father, Son, and Holy Spirit are caught up into the life of the Holy Trinity who now dwells within us. He who is one, true, good, and beautiful radiates from his immensity goodness upon all who seek him. As with the earthly father and his son, so our Heavenly Father loves us and desires our perfection. He loves us with the same Spirit in which he loves himself. We in turn respond lovingly to his benevolence, desire also to please him, and approach ever closer to him; because we love him in the same Spirit of love in which the Father loves the Son and the Son loves the Father. Divine adoption has made us sons of the Father and, thereby, brethren in Christ through the Holy Spirit.

This grace, whereby we participate in the life of the Holy Trinity, is ours in Christ Jesus (Jn. 16:15). It imprints our destiny and destines us for eternal life. From all eternity God has held us in his thoughts. We have no idea what we are meant to become. But God calls us to that perfection which is our inheritance in him. God has created us for eternity, that he may delight in us and we in him, with the same Spirit of love which is the communion of the Holy Trinity. It is through the divine indwelling that baptized Christians share the same dignity: we are brethren in Christ and, therefore, heirs to his kingdom, "for it has pleased the Father to give you the kingdom." This kingdom belongs to you who are one Spirit in Christ Jesus providing you persevere in love towards one another: the love which is the Spirit of God.

¹³ Enter by the narrow gate, since the road that leads to destruction is wide and spacious, and many take it; ¹⁴ but it is a narrow gate and a hard road that leads to life, and only a few find it. ¹⁵ Beware of false prophets who come to you disguised as sheep but underneath are ravenous wolves. ¹⁶ You will be able to tell them by their fruits. Can people pick grapes from thorns, or figs from thistles? ¹⁷ In the same way, a sound tree produces good fruit but a rotten tree bad fruit. ¹⁸ A sound tree cannot bear bad fruit, nor a rotten tree bear good fruit. ¹⁹ Any tree that does not produce good fruit is cut down and thrown on the fire. ²⁰ I repeat, you will be able to tell them by their fruits.

In the beatitudes Jesus has described those who are citizens of the kingdom, the nature of their blessedness, and their separation from the world. He then proceeded to guide us on how to surpass the duplicitous morality of this world in order to pursue the righteousness of the kingdom. Furthermore, he has explained how we may advance in the kingdom through the exercise of alms, prayer, and fasting which increases our holiness and keeps us in the presence of God. He has also admonished us against false judgements against our neighbour and fellow Christians, and enjoined us to ask, seek and knock in order to receive the gifts of the kingdom. But now to encourage us even more earnestly in the kingdom, Our Lord warns us of the difficulties attendant upon living out its ethos. He urges us to choose the narrow way by avoiding false teachers, those whose purpose is to turn us away from the kingdom and its righteousness in order to lure us onto the way of moral evil and spiritual destruction.

This choice between the two ways—one that leads to life and one that leads to death—is a universal teaching through all ages and across cultures, and is by no means atypical of Hebrew and Christian instruction either. "Today, look, I am offering you a blessing and a curse: a blessing if you obey the commandments of the LORD your God which I enjoin on you this day; a curse if you disobey the commandments of the LORD your God and leave the way which today I have marked out for you, by following other gods whom you have not known" (Dt. 11:26). This theme is elaborated more fully in Deuteronomy 30:15–19 where the choice is offered between life and prosperity, death and destruction, or blessing and curse; ending with the exhortation to: "Choose life, then, so that you and your descendents may live, by loving YHWH your God, obeying his voice, and holding fast to him; for in this your life consists."

The theme is continued in the wisdom literature. For example Psalm 1 contrasts the path of the upright which "like a tree planted near streams bears fruit in due season" with the way of sinners which is "like chaff blown about by the wind." The book of Proverbs provides several descriptions of this path of righteousness: Proverbs 4:18 compares it with the light of dawn increasing in brightness; while verse 25–27 warns not to turn to right or the left in order to keep one's feet from evil. More significantly Proverbs 5:6 and 15:24 call the path of righteousness "the path of life" contrasting it with the path that leads to Sheol. The book of Wisdom 5:6–7 contrasts the way of truth and uprightness with the way of lawlessness and destruction; and the way of the Lord with the trackless wilderness. The prophet, Jeremiah, invokes this choice between life and death in his warnings to Zedekiah the king of Judah (vs. 21:18).

Finally, it must be noted how the *Didache* in its first six chapters, with their numerous allusions to the sermon on the Mount, also describes Christian practice as the way of life in opposition to the way of death practised by those who follow wickedness, such as...

> murders, adulteries, lusts, fornications, thefts, idolatries, witchcraft, sorceries, robberies, perjuries, hypocrisies, duplicities, deceit, pride, malice, self-will, avarice, foul language, jealousy, insolence, arrogance, and boastfulness. Here are those who persecute good men, hold truth in abhorrence, and love falsehood. . . . Knowledge of their Creator is not in them; they do away with their infants and deface God's image; they turn away the needy and oppress the afflicted; they aid and abet the rich but arbitrarily condemn the poor; they are utterly and altogether sunk in iniquity. Flee my children from all of this!

How apparent are all these vices in our present culture! And how broad is this survey of the vices that constitute this culture of death! The *Didache* ends this section on the Way of Death with a stern warning similar to that of Our Lord concerning false prophets: "Beware that no one tempts you away from the path of this Teaching, for such a man's tuition can have nothing to do with God" (cp. 6). The *Didache* concludes by cautioning about dubious teachers and by suggesting how one can discriminate the true apostles and prophets from the false ones (11–13).

The thrust, therefore, of all these texts is that life is presented as a choice between two ways: one narrow and difficult and the other broad and easy. One leads to eternal life the other leads to destruction. One way requires loving God our Creator above all things, and our neighbour as our very selves; the other leads to love of the creature above the Creator and, therefore, ourselves above all. These two ways are offered to us as a choice we freely make. This serves to underscore yet again that Our Lord is affirming that we have both the free will and the intelligence to make this distinction. In the sobering and stark metaphor of the two ways, Jesus is reminding us of the opposition between our two natures in a manner similar to that of St. Paul:

> So, then, I discover this principle that when I want to do good, evil is present with me. For I delight in the law of God in my inner self; but I see in my members a different principle which battles with the law of my mind, making me captive to the law of sin that dwells in my members. O wretched man that I am! Who will rescue me from this body doomed to death? I thank God through Jesus Christ our Lord. (Ro. 7:21–25)

This is the perennial struggle of the Christian conscience between the concupiscence that leads us to destruction and the moral precepts that lead to salvation (*CCC* 1696, 1714).

Therefore, Our Lord's metaphor of the gate and the way is an allegory for the exclusiveness of admittance into his kingdom, as well as the difficulty of the struggle to remain on the righteous path to which the gate has given us access. The narrowness of the gate symbolizes the exclusive set of standards that leads to the difficult path of eternal life; while the wide gate represents the plentiful abundance of attractions that leads to destruction. The contrast between wide and narrow implies that one must divest oneself of vain and excessive worldly baggage (mammon) in order to pass through the narrow gate that leads onto the way which takes one into the kingdom. While the sinful person laden with all one's worldly attachments and accumulations is freely able to pass only through the wide gate.

The context of this sermon and its occasional nature indicate that the narrow way is the way of self-denial and obedience already outlined in the beatitudes and the elucidations given in the rest of the sermon. The path to destruction, on the other hand, is the opposite of that teaching. It is broad because the temptations to evil are diverse and indeterminable. It essentially represents the license to do what is right in one's own eyes (Gen. 3:5–6; Jg. 17:6; 21:25) which allows the maximum latitude to live as one desires, not as God approves (Pr. 14:12; 21:2). It is the way of self-indulgence and wilfulness. This way leads to destruction.

Our Lord is not explicit here about what that destruction ultimately entails, but it is clearly the contrary of eternal life in the kingdom. It can certainly be taken in the broad sense to refer to the personal destruction that sin brings to the soul and to the life of the sinner. But this fate also includes the more specific sense of eternal damnation which would be the unavoidable outcome for those remaining on that path. Such a penalty is the assured recompense presented throughout Matthew's gospel and the rest of the New Testament as well.[3]

In any case, according to the tradition of the Catholic Church and the Magisterium, the opposite of eternal life is eternal reprobation for those who persist in wickedness to the point that they would die impenitent: "Mortal sin is a radical possibility of human freedom. . . . If it is not redeemed by repentance and God's forgiveness, it causes exclusion from Christ's kingdom and the eternal death of hell, for our freedom has the power to make choices forever, with no turning back" (*CCC* 1861). It is as a person (body and soul) that one makes moral choices; and it is as a person, therefore, that the human individual is judged (2 Cor. 5:10). At the moment of death, when the soul leaves the body, one ceases to be a morally

---

3. Mt. 3:7; 5:22; 10:28; 13:42, 50; 18:9; 23:15, 33; Ro. 9:22; 1 Cor. 5:5; Phil. 3:19; 2 Th. 1:9; 2 Pt. 2:1; 3:16. See also: Mt. 5:29–30; 8:12; 22:13; 25:30, 41; Mk. 9:43, 45, 47; Lk. 12:5; Ro. 2:3; 14:10, 12; 2 Cor. 5:10; 2 Tim. 4:1; Heb. 6:2; 9:27; 10:31; 1 Pt. 4:5, 18; Rev. 19:20; 20; 10, 14–15.

integrated person;[4] and all opportunity for moral repentance also ceases until the reunification of body and soul at the final judgement (Heb. 9:27). But then it is too late. As we have seen earlier, God will neither abrogate nor override the free will he has given us: for that would be a morally repugnant disavowal of our intrinsic human nature, given to us by God himself in the beginning. Therefore, our free will has instilled us with the capacity to make those choices that eternally affect one's fate before God. It is the radical nature of free will that it is free to determine itself eternally. And God respects this. One can freely and finally refuse to enter the gate that leads to eternal life forever. This is *a fortiori* the terrible implication of "destruction" in Our Lord's meaning.

Those who find the narrow gate are few, while those who enter the gate leading to destruction are many. Taken in isolation, the Lord's saying does not stipulate the final proportion of the saved relative to the damned, because—as the metaphor permits—there is always the hope that some of the "many" will eventually submit to God's call and repent while they are still on the way. However, that there will be a relatively large proportion of the finally reproved cannot be entirely dismissed either: since "many will be called but few will be chosen" (Mt. 22:14). Nevertheless, this parable is a warning and an insistence that we remain in the proper path prescribed by Our Lord in his sermon, for there can be no possibility to choose after death. "The wages of sin is death, but the gift of God is eternal life in Christ Jesus our Lord" (Ro. 6:23).

The broad way is also the way of the false prophets. The scribes and the Pharisees are one example of these "blind guides" (Mt. 5:20; 23:16–26); but there are also other false prophets who will arise and deceive many (Mt. 24:11). These false prophets come clothed like sheep, but inwardly are ravenous (*arpages*: plundering, rapacious) wolves. The image of ravenous wolves comes from Genesis 49:27: "Benjamin is a ravening wolf, in the morning he devours the prey, in the evening he is still sharing out the spoil." A similar image

---

4. As the form of the body, the soul and body make a single morally autonomous human nature. The soul is made for the body which is the instrument through which she acts. Without the body the soul cannot accomplish her moral will.

occurs in Ezekiel 22:27 where the priests and leaders of Israel are lions and wolves tearing their prey and shedding blood to steal what belongs to the people. Throughout the gospels "sheep" always refers to Jesus' disciples, while Jesus refers to himself as the shepherd who protects his flock from wolves.[5]

All of these false prophets will be known by their fruits. Character reveals itself by its actions: "The good person out of the good treasure of one's heart produces good, and the evil person out of one's evil treasure produces evil; for out of the abundance of the heart the mouth speaks" (Lk. 6:45). It is clear from this passage from Luke's account of the sermon, and Our Lord's warning to beware of false prophets, that the meaning of fruits in this context is false teaching—what "the mouth speaks." The thrust of these metaphors is clear: The disciples who are walking on the narrow way must avoid false teachers who have insinuated themselves into the flock for the purpose of luring the disciples onto the broad path that leads to destruction. They disguise their teachings in an attractive form designed to deceive, but they cannot hide their moral characters. Their behavior betrays them as "blind guides" who would otherwise lead "many" into the pit. These are they who cause scandal and dissension within the Church. But, like thorns and thistles, their fate is to be eventually cut down and burned. Therefore, the prudent and assiduous disciple would do well to follow those who have produced the fruits worthy of eternal life. For us today these would most certainly have to include the saints and doctors of the Church.

[21] It is not anyone who says to me, "Lord, Lord," who will enter the kingdom of Heaven, but the person who does the will of my Father in Heaven. [22] When the day comes many will say to me, "Lord, Lord, did we not prophesy in your name, drive out demons in your name, work many miracles in your name?" [23] Then I shall tell them to their faces: I have never known you; away from me, all evil doers! [24] 'Therefore, everyone who listens to these words of mine and acts on them will be like a sensible man who built his house on rock. [25] Rain came down, floods rose, gales blew and

5. Mt. 10:16; 12:11–12; 26:31; Mk. 6:34; Lk. 15:4, 6; Jn. 10:1–16.

hurled themselves against that house, and it did not fall: it was founded on rock. ²⁶ But everyone who listens to these words of mine and does not act on them will be like a stupid man who built his house on sand. ²⁷ Rain came down, floods rose, gales blew and struck that house, and it fell; and what a fall it had!'

The matter of the divergent ways—the way of those who say, but do not do, and that of those who both hear and do—comes to a dramatic climax in this passage. From the beginning of the sermon, Our Lord has contrasted the path of true discipleship in the kingdom with the hypocrisy and disbelief of the world. The scribes and the Pharisees are but the personification of a duplicitous attitude which is always prevalent in the world, but is also a temptation constantly vexing the people of God. In the section labelled "antitheses" this problem is clearly articulated. But the issue continues to surface in the discourse on the three pillars of piety (alms, prayer, and fasting) as well as that concerning the serving of two masters and authentic vs. false judgement. This matter culminates in the definitive and irrevocable choice between one or other of the two ways.

Yet lest one should maintain that it is enough for the disciple on the narrow way merely to affirm the Lordship of Jesus or even to perform miracles in his name, thinking that these are the fruits which he intends, the Lord adds this final warning: "It is not anyone who says to me, 'Lord, Lord,' who will enter the kingdom of Heaven, but the one who does the will of my Father in Heaven." The fruits of true disciples are the performance of the will of Our Heavenly Father who providentially keeps us and who has sent his Son as the exemplar of that narrow way that leads to God.

The phrase "when the day comes" alludes, of course, to the terrible day of judgement, also known as the Day of the Lord. Many prophecies from the Old and New Testament describe the coming Day of the Lord.⁶ They present a composite spectacle of terrible plagues, catastrophic wars, and imminent judgement of the nations. The earliest, direct use of the phrase is in Isaiah: "For the day of the

6. Is. 2:12; 13:6, 9; 34:8; Ez. 13:5, 30:3; Joel 1:15, 2:1, 11, 31; 3:14; Amos 5:18, 20; Ob. 1:15; Zeph. 1:7, 8, 14; 2:3; Zech. 14:1; Mal. 4:5; Acts 2:20; 1 Cor. 5:5; 2 Cor. 1:14; Phil. 1:6; 1 Thess. 5:2; 2 Thess. 2:2; 2 Pt. 3:10. Cf. Rev. 6:17; 16:14.

LORD of hosts shall be upon every one that is proud and lofty, and upon every one that is lifted up; and he shall be brought low" (Isaiah 2:12). But the most complete description is given by the prophet Joel:

> Blow the ram's-horn in Zion,
> sound the alarm on my holy mountain!
> Let everybody in the country tremble,
> for the Day of the LORD is coming, yes, it is near.
> Day of darkness and gloom,
> Day of cloud and blackness.
> Like the dawn, across the mountains
> spreads a vast and mighty people,
> such as has never been before,
> such as will never be again
> to the remotest ages. (Joel 2:1–2)

> I shall show portents in the sky and on earth,
> blood and fire and columns of smoke.
> The sun will be turned into darkness,
> and the moon into blood,
> before the Day comes, that great and terrible Day.
> All who call on the name of the LORD will be saved. (Joel 3:1–5)

From the first mention of the expression Day of the Lord, the theme of a terrible epiphany of the "God who comes" is all too evident. Amos announces that, because of Israel's great evil, God's coming will signal for them disaster and peril: a day of darkness (5:18, 20). Preponderant in this divine intervention is the awesome presence of the Almighty. Human existence shrinks before this reality. On that day, "all hands will fall limp, every man's heart will melt in terror" (Is. 13:7). The peoples will fall into pain and convulsions. In stereotypical language the sun will refuse to give its light and the moon and the stars will cease to shine (Is. 13:10).

In the New Testament the Day of the Lord is identified with the coming of Jesus Christ: "I am quite confident that the One who began a good work in you will go on completing it until the Day of Jesus Christ" (Phil. 1:6). However, as in the Old Testament, that Day will be a time of judgement and it will come suddenly with disastrous finality: "The Lord is not being slow in carrying out his promises . . . rather he is being patient with you, wanting nobody to be lost and everybody to be brought to repentance. The Day of the Lord will come like a thief, and then with a roar the sky will vanish, the elements will catch fire and melt away, the earth and all that it contains will be burned up" (2 Pt. 3:9–10).

Without question, the Day of the Lord is the time of God's victory over evil and his vindication over the rebellious nations. The descriptions of the portents in the sky and on earth at the end of history are typologies of an epiphany of awesome power; for this is the Day when evil shall be eliminated at last and the wicked will receive their just recompense. On the other hand, the descriptions of God's blessing and the restoration of an Eden-like paradise are meant to offer hope for those whose trust is in the Lord God. The certain imminence of that day—with its ominous aspect of judgement as well as its anticipation of wondrous transformation encompassing human beings, society, the earth, and the whole heavens also—exhorts the people of God especially to continue to walk in the narrow path leading to eternal life.

But how desperate are the persons who merely called Jesus "Lord" but did not produce the works of righteousness which a sincere faith in Jesus necessitates! Their protestations—"did we not prophesy in your name, drive out demons in your name, work many miracles in your name?"—betray their astonishment. Although their question is designed in such a way as to gain some acknowledgement from Jesus, yet it affords them no advantage even though they did these things in his name. For although it is necessary that they would have had to have received the Holy Spirit in order to call Jesus Lord (1 Cor. 12:3), nevertheless, they did not do the will of the Heavenly Father in performing works from divine charity. We are reminded here of St. Paul's thesis in the thirteenth chapter of 1 Corinthians (vs. 2) that "though I have the power of prophecy, to penetrate all mysteries and knowledge, and though I have all faith necessary to move mountains—if I am without love I am nothing." It is not sufficient, therefore, merely to declare Jesus "Lord," if one does not show him obedience, for that is the very hypocrisy that Jesus has constantly denounced.

Nor must we assume that it is not possible to do miracles in Jesus' name unless one were a true and devoted disciple. In Acts 19:13–17 we read that the seven sons of a Jewish priest named Sceva had attempted to exorcise demons in the name of Jesus, to which the demon retorted: "Jesus I recognize, and Paul I know, but who are you?" Simon Magus tried the same thing (Acts 8:9–24). Even Jesus declared that false prophets and false Christs would arise in the last days who would perform signs and wonders enough to even deceive the elect, if it were possible (Mt. 24:24). "Yet do not rejoice that the spirits submit to you; rejoice instead that your names are written in Heaven" (Lk. 10:20).

However, because they did not perform acts of loving kindness but works of evil instead, they were cast out from the presence of the Lord. The "evil doers" are those who failed to respond to the demands of the Sermon on the Mount, and who tried to use their association with the "Lord" to their own advantage. (See Mt. 22: 11–13; 25:11–12; 25:41–46; Lk. 13:26–27.) The point is that merely confessing oneself to be a disciple of Jesus is not enough: one must be obedient to his will which is also the will of his heavenly Father. Some of Jesus' followers may have had all the charisms mentioned by St. Paul, but they lacked the sanctifying grace of the Holy Spirit, whose fruits are acts of loving kindness. Those persons are not *of* the kingdom of God. The way of the kingdom embodies the beatitudes; practising a superior righteousness by curbing anger and lust, respecting marital fidelity, meaning and keeping one's word, receiving insults with patience, and loving one's enemies; performing alms, prayer, and fasting in a genuine spirit and not for attention; and refraining from condemning others. Those who do not do these things from a pure heart, but who, dissembling, feign themselves to be members of the kingdom, will be weeded out like the wheat and the tares (Mt. 13:30), or like the useless fish in the net (13:49), or the badly attired wedding guest (22:10), or the foolish virgins (25:12), or the man who buried his talents (25:30).

Yet as clearly and as often as Jesus has declared that none who do not possess the kingdom of God within, from a pure heart or devout spirit, shall enter the kingdom of Heaven; nevertheless Our Blessed Lord knew that many would not receive this saying. Therefore, he once more affirms that "*many* shall say in that day, Lord, Lord. . . ." Thus he calls to mind those "many" who have chosen the broad way that leads to destruction. They are many, not few: for they have not been found among the poor in spirit, the meek, the pure in heart; they have not mourned for the kingdom or hungered and thirsted for righteousness, practised mercy, or promoted peace. Nor have they patiently endured the persecutions that are the inevitable lot of the *anawim*, but rather have succumbed before the storm like a house built upon the sand. They have been enticed by the world, the flesh, and the devil, having chosen to serve the "lord mammon" instead, and in so doing they have denied their true Lord and Savior.

Their hypocrisy is all the more grave when contrasted with the clear claim to divinity which Jesus asserts: for their infidelity is opposed to the Son of God! Jesus has proclaimed himself as the Lord of the Last Judgement in whose name one's eternal fate and destiny is determined. His authority in Heaven and earth is revealed in his having identified himself as the God who judges on the Day of the Lord: "When the day comes many will say to me.... Then I shall tell them." Already here, early in Jesus' ministry, he claims nothing less than being the One to whom the entire world, believers and unbelievers, would be accountable.

Furthermore, Jesus reveals in this passage that he is in a unique sense God's Son; for he says "my Father." Jesus is always careful to distinguish the term "my Father" from "your Father."[7] For example in John 20:17 just before his ascension, when Jesus says to Mary of Magdala "I am ascending to my Father and your Father," he shows that he perceived himself to be the Son of God in a special sense.

It can be proved from many other passages in scripture that Jesus was conscious of his divine Sonship. For example: in an early saying from what scholars have called Q, we have an authentic personal testimony of Jesus own consciousness: "All things have been delivered to me by my Father; and no one knows the Son except the Father, and no one knows the Father except the Son and any one to whom the Son chooses to reveal him" (Mt. 11:27 = Lk. 10:22). Also, Jesus is aware of possessing a dignity which is above that of men and

---

7. Mt. 5:45, 48; 6:9, 14, 15, 18; 10: 32, 33; 11:27; 12:50; 16:27; 18:10, 14, 35; 26:29, 53; Jn. 8:19, 49; 10:38; 12:49; 14:7 ff.; 15;24; 17:25.

angels. He is aware of surpassing the prophets and kings of Israel, Jonah and Solomon, Moses and Elijah (Mt. 12:41ff.; 17:3; Mk 9:4; Lk. 9:30). He claims authority over the angels who are his ministers and who will accompany him at his second coming (Mt. 4:11, 13:41, 16:27, 24:31, 26:53). Like God he sends out prophets, seers, and teachers of the law giving them "a mouth and wisdom, which no adversary can withstand" (Mt. 23:34; Lk. 21:15). He exercises the authority of altering or even nullifying the precepts of the law given to Moses, even to proclaiming himself Lord of the Sabbath (Mt. 5:21; 12:8). He establishes a new covenant with his community, imposing upon his disciples obligations which only God can demand, namely absolute love for him to the extent of demanding good works on his behalf and even of dying for him (Mt. 26:28; Mt. 10:37–39; 25:31–36). And as if this were not enough to convince one, Our Lord applies to himself the sacred name (YHWH) in his repeated use of the phrase I AM, *ego eimi*: "Truly, truly, I say to you before Abraham was, I Am" (Jn. 8:28, 58; 13:19).

Indeed, the closeness of the relationship between Jesus and his heavenly Father cannot be better expressed than in his *high priestly prayer* to God (Jn. 17):

> Father, the hour has come; glorify thy Son that the Son may glorify thee.... I glorified thee on earth, having accomplished the work which thou gavest me to do; and now, Father, glorify thou me in thy own presence with the glory which I had with thee before the world was made.
>
> I have manifested thy name to the men whom thou gavest me out of the world.... Now they know that everything that thou hast given me is from thee; for I have given them the words which thou gavest me, and they have received them and know in truth that I came from thee; and they have believed that thou didst send me.
>
> The glory which thou hast given to me I have given to them, that they may be one even as we are one, I in them and thou in me, that they may become perfectly one, so that the world may know that thou hast sent me and hast loved them even as thou hast loved me....
>
> O righteous Father, the world has not known thee, but I have known thee; and these know that thou hast sent me. I made known

to them thy name, and I will make it known, that the love with
which thou hast loved me may be in them, and I in them.

Jesus has revealed an intimacy with God which is not known by the
world and an authority to unite his community to him and to God
based precisely upon that loving relationship that he has with his
heavenly Father. He is aware of possessing a glorified, pre-existent
relationship with God that he wants to manifest to those whom
God has entrusted to him. He attests that in his Person he has
revealed to his flock the very name of God.

Finally, Jesus is conscious of possessing supreme authority—"All
authority in heaven and on earth has been given to me" –commissioning his apostles to make disciples of all nations, baptizing them
in the name of the Son (which he associates with the names of God
the Father and His Holy Spirit) and teaching them to observe *his*
commandments (Mt. 28:18). This authority is further manifested
through his capacity of bestowing upon others the power to heal
and exorcise demons in his name (Mt. 10:1, 8; Lk. 9:1; 10:17). Yet
even more wonderful is his awareness that his personal sacrifice will
serve to atone for the sins of others (Mt. 20:28; 26:28) and that he
would be with his disciples to the end of the age (Mt. 28:20).

Jesus is conscious of a profound relationship with his Father even
from before the foundation of the world; he bases the authority for
all he says and does on this awareness; and he even goes to his death
to confirm and exemplify this relationship. Jesus is aware of a
unique and divine relationship with his heavenly Father. He is
properly and rightly called and *is* the Son of the Father, his eternally
generated self-expression.

Therefore, it is no surprise that Our Lord Jesus claims for himself
the authority to judge the world on the great Day of the Lord: that
he establishes himself (and the truth that he reveals) as the criterion
for entry into the kingdom, and, therefore, the rightful eschatological judge. And it is no surprise that Jesus has selected hypocrisy as
the sin which more than any other evokes such opprobrium from
him (Mt. 23). Whether it is the scribes and the Pharisees, the money
changers in the Temple, or the lukewarm Laodiceans whom he
spews from his mouth, if there is any sin that Jesus detests most, it is
the sin of hypocrisy or duplicity in those who feign belief, and then

deny him by refusing to obey.

However, it is the sensible ones who listen and act, who build their house on the rock, who will be able to endure the storms and deluge of persecutions which inevitably befall the Christian. So how are we to understand the word "rock" in this instance? It is most certainly not merely confessing that Jesus is Lord. While such a confession is necessary for salvation, yet it is, *from the very lips of Jesus*, not sufficient: "Not everyone who says 'Lord, Lord' will enter the kingdom of Heaven, but the one who does the will of my Father in Heaven." Theologians may make subtle and necessary distinctions concerning faith and works, but what humble devoted disciple would presume upon the Father by calling Jesus "Lord" only to go off to do whatsoever one pleased? Common sense knows better than that (Ro. 3:31; 6:1–4, 15–19). Love does better than that (Jn. 14:15). Only a faith that produces the fruits of righteousness can save (Ro. 2:6–16). Hypocrisy cannot. One cannot call Jesus "Lord" and then disobey the Father whose Word incarnates the Son.

Therefore, while it is true that Christ Jesus is the rock upon which the house of our faith is built (1 Cor. 10:4), it must be understood that this involves not just his saving act alone, but all that he exemplifies and accomplishes. Christ is the substance of the Father and the incarnation of his Wisdom. It is all of Christ—his Person, life, teaching, passion, death, and resurrection—which is the rock upon which one's own life must be structured. It is also the Church which he founded built upon the rock of St. Peter whose office in turn rests upon Jesus himself who appointed him to this service; and to which he promised to give his Holy Spirit who would lead her into all truth. In fine, the rock is the whole Christ and all he brings and commends to us for our salvation: he cannot be sundered from himself.

Nor can the Son be separated from all that his Holy Spirit has wrought in the people of God throughout salvation history and tradition. It is the *anawim* who will manifest the gifts of his Holy Spirit: wisdom, understanding, counsel, knowledge, piety, fortitude, and fear of the Lord (Is. 11:2). These are the virtues that will enable them to withstand the tumult of the rains, the flood, and the gales; i.e., the temptations of the world, the flesh, and the devil. For the world will rain down upon them its falsehoods and its entice-ments; and the flesh will flood their souls with desire; and the devil will breathe his lies and rage his taunts. But the house built upon the rock founded upon the Christ will be the one standing at the Day of the Lord. These are the sensible ones who hear the word of the Lord and act on it. "Blessed are those who are persecuted for righteousness sake, for theirs is the kingdom of Heaven."

> [28] Jesus had now finished what he wanted to say, and the crowds were astonished at his teaching, [29] because he taught them as one who had authority, unlike their own scribes.

Jesus taught with an authority unlike that of the scribes, who were the equivalent of our biblical scholars of today. Unlike the scribes—who perennially base their authority on their reputations, qualifica-tions, or methods of argumentation—Jesus' authority is sure because of Who he is. All truth is contingent upon the Eternal Word; no truth can ever contradict it.[8] Within that narrow compass of what is self-evident to the first principles of our intellects, created in the image of God, there is a degree of certainty. But wander too far from these narrow confines, and it is not surprising that the definitive history of human thought "would have to be the history of its successive regrets and its impotencies."[9] Happily, however, when "Wisdom has built herself a house" ... "the gates of the underworld shall not prevail against it." Our faith in the incarnate Son assures us of this.

On Mount Eremos Wisdom delighted to hold counsel among her

---

8. This implies that there can be no autonomous, self-authenticating human authority for argumentation. It has been proved by Kurt Gödel that: all formal sys-tems will eventually produce propositions whose consistency cannot be decided from within that system itself. Therefore, one cannot presume upon the internal consistency of a philosophical system in order to validate its axioms. Merely deny its axioms and the formal system collapses. Also the theorems of Church, Turing, and Chaitin extend Gödel's theorems to algorithmic methods. It would seem that St. Thomas erred when he taught that the separate sciences can exist independently of theology; while St. Bonaventure contended that all human arts must be shown to be reducible to revealed theology in order to be valid.

9. Albert Camus, *The Myth of Sisyphus*. Cf. Ps. 94:11; Is. 29:14; 1 Co. 1:19–20; 3:19–20.

children. And like the crowd we too are astonished. For the authority which we have encountered is no less than the *Shekinah*, the
vision of the presence of God. Christ Jesus is the glory of the effulgence of his Heavenly Father. From the eternal utterance of the
Father proceeds his Word, which emanates immediately from his
substance: a real, complete, natural, and well-defined image of God;
fully and perfectly expressing and containing his reality, nature,
excellence, majesty, perfection, and divinity. Such resplendence of
form adorned Jesus' sacred humanity with magisterial grace, ten-
derness and forgiveness; innocence and beauty, benevolence and
truth. All perfections stream from Our Lord, radiating his splen-
dour. "How beautiful upon the mountains are the feet of him . . .
who says to Zion 'Your God is King'!" (Is. 52:7).

Epilogue
On Being a Disciple

And there shall come forth a shoot out of the root of Jesse, and a flower shall grow from his roots. And the spirit of the LORD shall rest upon him: the spirit of wisdom and of understanding, the spirit of counsel and of fortitude, the spirit of knowledge and of godliness. And he shall be filled with the spirit of the fear of the LORD (Isaiah 11:1–3).

C ENTRAL TO THE TEACHING of Jesus is what it means to belong to the kingdom of Heaven and how one may seek it. The beatitudes begin by describing those who truly belong to his kingdom and the blessings vouchsafed to them. They are salt and light to the world. By assiduously fulfilling the precepts of the kingdom they exceed worldly righteousness. It is also apparent from the prayer Jesus taught that the kingdom is to be prayed for as a fulfilment of the will of the Father: a treasure to be sought for all peoples on earth. And as a result of the dignity which the kingdom confers, one can place one's trust wholeheartedly in the omniscient providence of the Father who governs his kingdom with meticulous care. Finally, the kingdom is an exclusive dominion which is to be sought earnestly and with deep spiritual sincerity, for the way is difficult and is tread only by the few.

Jesus himself is the quintessential figure of the kingdom; for the trials and persecutions, which shall befall those belonging to the kingdom, are regarded as being suffered for his sake. Jesus' unparalleled centrality as the initiator and consummator of the kingdom connotes this Christ-centred emphasis. Jesus did not intend his sermon solely to rest on an ethical platform merely, but upon the messianic promise inherent in the nature of the kingdom. The good news of the kingdom is spoken of clearly and concisely, with the desire that some will repent and come to the knowledge of the truth. And that truth is Christ himself in all his effulgence, beauty, majesty, and glory. He brings with him the kingdom and manifests it in every movement of his sacred Person: for he embodies the kingdom since he is one substance with the Father and the Holy Spirit.

Jesus' discourse is not to be received merely ethically—although that tropological sense should not be underemphasized. Rather, the sermon's meaning should surge from its Christocentric depths. But what then is the depth of Christ's Being if not the consubstantial life he shares with his Father in the Holy Spirit? It is from here that the four senses of understanding emerge. Jesus is the incarnate Word of God who emanates from the Father in the Holy Spirit, so that the literal, moral, Christological, and mystical senses have their grounding in him. Jesus stands on the mountain in the literal-historical sense; the incarnate Word teaches us about the righteousness of the kingdom and its moral sense; but he manifests its ethos also in his Person as the Christ; and invites us into the deepest mysteries of the kingdom through his Holy Spirit who leads us into all truth.

Thus without the indwelling of the Holy Spirit we cannot enter into the mysteries of the kingdom: "anyone who does not have the Spirit of Christ does not belong to him" (Ro. 8:9). And "no one can say 'Jesus is Lord' except by the Holy Spirit" (1 Cor. 12:14). Nevertheless by virtue of our baptism we are the temples of the Holy Spirit (1 Cor. 3:16). Through the Spirit's permanent and personal indwelling in our souls, given to us at baptism, the Holy Spirit continually communicates to each of us the intimate life of the Triune God. This life originates in the Father as its principle and is offered to us in the Son who is its form. "God has sent the Spirit of his Son into our hearts, crying *"Abba!* Father!"" (Gal. 4:6). This indwelling pertains to all three divine Persons, but it is attributed, by appropriation, to the Holy Spirit by Jesus Christ himself. So we know that this indwelling is assuredly founded and wonderfully efficacious for the communication to us of that life which will render us genuine citizens of the kingdom of Heaven. It cannot be otherwise, for the Spirit which proceeds from the Father brings to us the Son whom the Father loves; and, returning as the love of the Son in us for the

Father, glorifies the Father. And, being sanctified by his Spirit, we too are made a holy offering to his beloved Father (Jn. 16:13–14; 17:17–23).

In order for us to act and grow in the beatitudes, this supernatural life to which we are called requires in us faculties of a similar divine character. This is the supernatural organism which includes the infused cardinal and theological virtues as well as the seven gifts of the Holy Spirit. Ever since Jerome's translation of the vulgate, these gifts have been identified as seven: wisdom, understanding, counsel, fortitude, knowledge, piety, and holy fear. These gifts complete and perfect the virtues and make the faithful disciple docile in readily obeying divine inspirations (*CCC* 1831). St. Thomas has said of these gifts that "the gifts are more perfect than the moral and intellectual virtues."[1] Reason and natural virtue can only take us so far in the holy life, but in order to progress to the perfection to which Christ has called us we need the supernatural gifts.

These seven gifts are able to bring to completion each of the beatitudes. For it has been a constant tradition since at least the fifth century and promoted by St. Augustine and St. Thomas that these seven gifts can be linked to each of the seven beatitudes. St. Augustine says in the *Catena Aurea*: "The number of these sentences should be carefully attended to; to these seven degrees of blessedness agree the operation of that seven-form Holy Spirit which Isaiah described. But as He began from the highest, so here He begins from the lowest; for there we are taught that the Son of God will descend to the lowest; here that man will ascend from the lowest to the likeness of God."[2] So these gifts are listed in a descending order headed by wisdom, which is the most excellent of the gifts since it is analogous to the nature of the Son of God who is himself incarnate Wisdom. Also, since "the fear of the Lord is the beginning of wisdom" (Pr. 9:10; Ps. 110:10), then it follows that holy fear is properly placed as lowest in the series and accordingly will be the first on our ascent in blessedness.

---

1. *Summa Theol.* IIa IIae q. 9, a. 2, ad. 3.
2. Quoted in St. Thomas Aquinas, *Catena Aurea,* Gospel of St. Matthew, ch. 5:3.

The fear of the Lord and spiritual poverty. The poor in spirit are the people of God, the *anawim*, who at the beginning of their spiritual journey recognize their need for God. They have found the treasure in the field, the pearl of great price, so that they are prepared to surrender all they have to purchase the kingdom. They realize that in order to become perfect they must detach themselves from everything that would compete with their devotion to God. "If you wish to be perfect, go and sell your possessions and give the money to the poor, and you will have treasure in Heaven; then come, follow me" (Mt. 19:21). They renounce mammon and choose to serve God only (Lk. 14:33). Realizing that mammon has its power over them because of the pride of ownership of one's possessions, therefore, the poor in spirit embrace their poverty for the sake of the Holy Spirit. "For as all other vices, but chiefly pride, cast down to hell; so all other virtues, but chiefly humility, conduct to Heaven; it is proper that he that humbles himself should be exalted" (Pseudo-Chrysostom). Thus the disciple begins at once at the root, pulling up pride which is the root of all evil, planting the seed of humility instead. "For everything that is in the world, the lust of the flesh, and the lust of the eyes, and the pride of life, is not of the Father, but is from the world" (1 Jn. 2:16).

A profound humility is at the source of that filial fear based upon a reverence and awe of God. This is not a question of fear of punishment because of past sins, nor of fear of hell, since the poor in spirit are already conscious of their need and desire of God. Rather, precisely because God is their greatest treasure, they dread any offence that may destroy the life of God in them. Their fear of displeasing God is born of a filial love for him; otherwise they would not be so anxious to remain in his grace. Thus holy fear begins the process of purgation by detaching us from those pleasures which would separate us from God. The gift of fear, being the first gift of the Holy Spirit, inclines our wills to a reverence for God and detaches us from anything which displeases him.

The gift of fear cultivates the cardinal virtue of temperance; firstly because it gives us a vivid sense of the sanctity and holiness of God, which culminates in the love of God for himself alone and in the need to glorify him in all that we say, do, feel, and think. As a consequence, one finds in oneself that the three desires spoken of by St. John above begin to diminish as the things of the world lose their allure, since the soul can find only her joy and satisfaction in God alone. Thirdly, because the essence of filial fear is based upon an exalted apprehension of God's majesty and immensity, the disciple develops a profound humility, confessing one's nothingness before God and declaring one's dependence upon him for all the good things he has given. Finally, like a gentle breeze wafting over the perfumed meadow, there arises in one a burgeoning impression of the beauty of the grace of the Holy Spirit. For love leads to light and the light of the Spirit is the face of the Son, who looks upon the Father, in whom all life is completed and in whom all motion rests. In him every creature is perfected for he is the principle and creator of all that is. Gentleness pervades the soul and spreads over all the things of the earth:

> Flowers appear on the earth,
> the season of glad songs has come,
> the cooing of the turtledove is heard in our land.
> The fig tree forms its first figs
> and the blossoming vines yield their fragrance.
> Come then, my beloved,
> my lovely one, come. (*Song of Songs*: 2:12–13)

Because all the gifts of the Holy Spirit are under his control and determination, they cannot be merited or actuated by us. Nevertheless, we can make ourselves receptive to the gift of holy fear by cultivating a love of solitude, recollection, mental prayer, and especially the practice of the presence of God. Brother Lawrence advises: "That we ought to give ourselves up entirely to God, with regard both to things temporal and spiritual, and seek our satisfaction only in the fulfilling of his will, whether he lead us by suffering or by consolation; for all would be equal to a soul resigned." True spiritual poverty rests in this self-abandonment to God, receiving with equanimity and serenity all that he sends us, realizing that he can do nothing evil, but that all things are for our good and the glory of his name. To arrive at such resignation we must be vigilant in keeping custody of the senses and making little acts for the love of God and the salvation of sinners. As we frequently turn to God during the day, crowning all our acts with sweet praises and expressions of love, so our love for him will be nourished and strengthened. Our love for creatures will diminish and everything will be properly ordered.

The fourteenth century Dominican mystic, Joannes Tauler, once encountered a beggar who was lying at the door to the church. When Tauler learned of the intimate union with God which the beggar had attained, he enquired of him: "Where did you find God?" The beggar answered: "Where I left creatures." Blessed are the poor in spirit, for theirs is the kingdom of Heaven.

The gift of piety and the Beatitude of meekness. The disciple, who has placed all trust in God's majesty, now bows before him in meekness and serenity. All presumption having passed, the disciple is blessed with a quiet confidence in God's providence, and gentleness pervades the earth. This still, quiet confidence in God is the source of meekness in the soul. It enables the disciple to rest quietly and securely in the providence of God which is also one's strength. With her house built firmly upon the rock of Christ Jesus, nothing can disturb one's soul; and from this solid foundation emerges a confident security so that one can afford to be gentle and gracious to all. "When I have learned contentment in poverty," St. Ambrose says, "the next lesson is to govern my heart and temper." Any possible irascibility or irritation at some offence is cut off at its source by meekness. In fact, perfected by the gift of piety, the soul not only renounces retaliation, but welcomes with wondrous serenity the injury received. Why? Because meekness comes precisely from that self-possession characteristic of genuine nobility: for the disciple has intimated that one's true dignity comes from having been made the adopted son of the Father through the Holy Spirit.

Noblesse oblige so we are told, but the nobility of the *anawim* is of such a high order and esteemed character that generosity, responsibility, and graciousness naturally flow from the sense of belonging to the august family of God. "All who are guided by the Spirit of God are sons of God; for what you received was not the spirit of slavery to bring you back into fear; you received the Spirit of adoption enabling us to cry out 'Abba, Father!' The Spirit himself joins with our spirit to bear witness that we are children of God. And if we are children then we are heirs: heirs of God and joint-heirs with Christ...." (Ro. 8:14–17). This nobility is one's inheritance because of one's adoption into the kingdom of God.

Piety, *pietas,* has its historical origins in the debt of gratitude we owe to our parents, our family, and our country. It comprises the loyalty of obligations that these evoke in us because of our sense of justice. Indeed, it is the virtue of justice—of giving to someone what is one's due—that is the basis of natural piety. But the supernatural gift of piety develops in us a deep filial affection and devotion to God. We are anxious to render to God the honour, glory, and reverence due to him, for we are his children. The gift of piety sanctifies the natural virtue of religion because it enables us to fulfil our religious duties with joy and fervor.

Thus the supernatural gift of piety arouses in the will a filial affection to God as Father and a tender devotion towards those persons and objects consecrated to him. Reverence for holy objects, relics, sacramentals, the Eucharist, priests, religious, and one's brothers and sisters in Christ marks the soul graced by this gift. The soul loves the Blessed Virgin, the angels, and the saints and develops pious devotions to them. One has a generous love towards the souls in purgatory for whom prayers and satisfactions are offered. One also has a deep friendship and reverence towards the Holy Father as the Vicar of Christ and visible head of the Church militant.

Holy piety elicits in us adoration of the ineffable mystery of the divine paternity in the Holy Trinity; for we ourselves are now caught up by the Holy Spirit into this communion. We are embraced in the love in which the Fatherhood of God generates the Son, and in which the Son loves the Father. This life is in us: this divine procession is our substance. We are not made of this divine substance, of course; but that life, which is ours in the Holy Spirit, *is* one substance with God the Father and God the Son. That is our nobility as temples of the Holy Spirit.

As a result we have a profound confidence in our Heavenly Father. We are no longer anxious about the things of this world: what we shall eat, what we shall wear. We are not concerned with health or sickness, length or shortness of life, persecution or praise, or success or failure. "For I am certain of this: neither death nor life, nor angels, nor principalities, nothing already in existence and nothing still to come, nor any power, nor the heights nor the depths, nor any created thing whatsoever, will be able to come between us and the love of God, known to us in Christ Jesus our Lord" (Ro. 8:38–39). Nothing is capable of disturbing your soul's peace: for you rest in God as a child in its Father's embrace.

This is consequent upon the supernatural gift of piety. Therefore, it is essential if we are to travel the way of sanctity that we render ourselves susceptible to this gift by cultivating spiritual childhood, for "Truly I say to you, unless you be converted, and become as little children, you shall not enter into the kingdom of Heaven" (Mt. 18:3). For those who are pure in spirit, the recognition that they are like children wholly dependent upon their heavenly Father has already taken root in them. Therefore, to dispose ourselves further to this gift, it is only necessary that we remind ourselves that nothing is sufficient of itself, but only in God who sustains all things in being. Give God the glory for everything, trusting in his mercy; thanking him ahead of time for all that he will give you. The Venerable Franciscan, Father Solanus Casey, doorkeeper, mystic, and who possessed remarkable gifts of healing and prophecy, offers this advice on spiritual *pietas*.[3]

> Why not foster confidence in God's divine Providence by humbly and in all childlike humility venturing to remind him in the person of our divine brother, Jesus, that we are his children. We should remind him that we are, and at least want to be reckoned, as among his "little ones." Therefore, we should thank him frequently for, not only the blessings of the present, but thank him ahead of time for whatever he foresees is pleasing to him that we suffer. We should do this not only in general, but in each particular case. We should leave everything absolutely in his divine disposal, including with all its circumstances, when, where, and how he may be pleased to dispose the events of our death.

Thus the gift of piety perfects meekness because it helps to situate all our actions and holy sentiments under the roof of the Father-

3. Quoted in Michael H. Crosby, *Thank God Ahead of Time* (Cincinnati: St. Anthony Messenger Press, 2009), citation page.

hood of God. All Christians need this gift if they are joyfully and readily to fulfil their duties of religion towards God, the saints, and the Church. Otherwise the tendency is to regard God as a master instead of a loving Father, prayer a burden rather than a comfort, and the trials and tribulations of life as unjust punishments or torments, while they are really opportunities for perseverance, patience, and satisfaction. These also dispose us to receive condign merit, since these works are performed consequent to an action of the Holy Spirit, and thereby increase our friendship with God.

The soul becomes meek because God is meek. Meekness makes us pleasing to God because it makes us like Jesus: "Learn from me, for I am meek and humble of heart; and you will find rest for your souls" (Mt. 11:29). And because all things belong to Christ, then they are yours also, "All things are yours; and you are Christ's and Christ is God's" (1 Cor. 3:22–23). As St. John of the Cross affirms: "Mine are the heavens and mine is the earth. Mine are the nations, the just are mine, and mine the sinners. The angels are mine, and the Mother of God, and all things are mine; and God himself is mine and for me, because Christ is mine and all for me." [4] The meek are truly blessed, for they shall have the earth for an inheritance, and even more: "Come, you *who my Father has blessed, take as your inheritance the kingdom* prepared for you since the foundation of the world" (Mt 25:34).

The gift of knowledge and those who mourn. The soul who has detached herself from mammon and who is at peace in the family of the Triune God now sees things under a celestial light. She no longer travels in darkness alone, but walks with the light of the Holy Spirit whose brilliance shines without obstruction over the entire extent of her life, penetrating to its depths, and revealing its secrets. The soul has received the supernatural gift of knowledge which by the illumination of the Holy Spirit gives her knowledge of created things in their relation to God. Everything is seen *sub specie aeternitatis,* as sacramental signs of the divine perfections. Both in the heavens and upon the earth God reveals something of what he is in himself.

4. *Sayings of Light and Love,* 27.

The heavens declare the glory of God,
the vault of heaven proclaims his handiwork,
day to day discourses of it,
night to night hands on the knowledge.
No utterance at all, no speech,
not a sound to be heard,
but from the entire earth the design stands out,
this message reaches the whole world. (Ps. 19:1–4)

For all creation receives, according to its nature and limits, the perfections communicated to it by the Creator. The world is a sym-
phony to God. With a single glance one intuits the singular and
sublime Cause of all things; and in ecstasy ascends to silent adoration. Before one's astonished eyes one's own wretchedness is also
laid bare: we have fallen so far short. And we are bathed with tears
of bitterness, as well as of gratitude for God's mercy and goodness.
On the one hand our souls recognize that all things of the earth are
vanity and affliction of spirit; for we have died to the world. But
simultaneously our souls realize, on the other hand, that our life is
hid with Christ in God (Col. 3:3). So tears of sorrow become per-
fused with joy. The soul weeps for the earth, for humanity, and for
the love of God.

Of course, the soul possessed God before she wept—one has had
the divine indwelling since baptism. But there was no room under
her roof for divine grace until such time as the soul emptied herself
so as to make way for the spiritual gifts. The door of her mansions
was closed to withhold its contents, while the real Treasure stood
outside knocking. But only until the soul arose, left her possessions,
and opened up to his Blessed Spirit, could she receive the consolation of being filled with the light of God.

The gift that makes all this possible is the gift of knowledge.
Under this gift the individual transcends discursive thinking, judging created things by a superior light. This right judging of creatures
is appropriately called the "science of the saints" because it sees all
things as ordered to God and judges them according to the perfections placed in them by God. Things are no longer ordered according to their advantage for oneself, but rather for the glory of God.
And because all things are seen as belonging to God and for the dif-

fusion of his glory, they are also regarded charitably, to be ordered equally for the benefit of all the children of God. For if all things belong to God, and the holy soul seeks the glory of God, then all things are subordinated to his disposition.

Because the soul sees the vanity of clinging to worldly things—that they tend to pervert us by enslaving us and diverting our attention from God—and perceives that they exist instead to manifest the perfections of God and to be used for his glory, the holy soul is able to raise one's spirit to the contemplation of their Creator. Now that God is increasingly becoming the centre of one's being, everything is seen from the divine perspective in the light of the Holy Spirit. Our natural capacity to grasp the form of things is elevated and sharpened so that we immediately are moved to perceive the beauty which God has placed in even the lowliest thing, and from this imperfect reflection of divine beauty our spirit is lifted to infinite beauty itself.

The soul properly enlightened by the sanctity of the Spirit learns repentance and sorrow for past sins. This follows logically from the preceding, since the soul now sees everything in its proper light, and therefore realizes how often creatures have been misused and how God's children have been abused by her in the past. But through the supernatural gift of knowledge one acquires a deeper respect and higher estimation for the things of God. And this combined with the virtue of piety makes one truly ashamed of how one has so scornfully treated the good things of the Father's house.

These are the principal effects of the gift of knowledge for which we must continue to seek. However, in addition to a love of solitude, recollection, mental prayer, and the practice of the presence of God, which are the ordinary means of disposing oneself to the gifts of the Holy Spirit, there are special means one can adopt to render oneself susceptible to the gift of knowledge. They all arise from the lights with which we have already been gifted.

First, we must continue to reflect upon the vanity and futility of worldly things. Often the world will betray its absurdity to us while we are going about our daily affairs or while observing the media with its vacuous milieu. These are opportunities to distance ourselves spiritually from their influence and to raise our thoughts to holy things: "whatsoever things are true, whatsoever things are honest, whatsoever things are just, whatsoever things are pure, whatsoever things are lovely, whatsoever things are of good report; if there be any virtue, and if there be any praise, think on these things" (Phil. 4:8).

Secondly, we should question our culture and our conditioning. We should ask ourselves of just what we are certain and what is of essential value; and avoid the falsehoods with which the world attempts to indoctrinate us. This requires constant vigilance. "Keep sober and alert, because your enemy the devil is on the prowl like a roaring lion, looking for someone to devour" (1 Pt. 5:8). On the contrary, we should try to perceive the hand of God in the governance of the world: how he brings to futility the works of man: "For God will bring every act to judgement, everything which is hidden, whether it is good or evil" (Eccl. 12:14). Our Heavenly Father cares for us with a loving providence, and he knows far better than we what is good for us. And although we may not always discern his secret design within all things, nevertheless we know that he is guiding and keeping us along that narrow way that will bring us to his everlasting kingdom. So we have no reason to fear anything from the world, for there is nothing concealed that will not be disclosed, nor hidden that will not be made known (Mt. 10:26).

Finally, let us cultivate that simplicity which sees everything as if for the first time. Nature has been transfigured for us by this gift of knowledge which lets us perceive the tracery of God in all things. Everything has a meaning because it speaks to us of God singing the praise of his perfections. This is the wonder of the innocent, the delight of the child, the joy of the mendicant wayfarer.

> All praise be yours, my Lord, through Brothers Wind and Air,
>> And fair and stormy, all the weather's moods,
>> By which you cherish all that you have made.
> All praise be yours, my Lord, through Sister Water,
>> So useful, lowly, precious, and pure.
> All praise be yours, my Lord, through Brother Fire,
>> Through whom you brighten up the night.
>
>> (St. Francis of Assisi)

If we can learn to see things in this manner then everything will become a ladder by which we may ascend to the love of God and praise him for the consolations which this marvellous gift brings to us. For even though we may mourn and shed copious tears for our wretchedness and for the futility of the disordered world of fallen humankind, nevertheless how much more prominent is the divine beauty in contrast. And though we yearn in this vale of tears for the final fulfilment of the promises of the kingdom, yet we still rejoice because of God's merciful bounty. We who mourn here are truly happy even so, because of the joy and hope which the gift of knowledge brings us. Blessed are they who mourn, for they shall be comforted.

The gift of fortitude and the hunger for justice. "As soon as I have wept for my sins," St. Ambrose points out, "I begin to hunger and thirst after righteousness. He who is afflicted with any sort of disease hath no hunger." Having received the gift of knowledge the disciple has become illuminated by the insight into the perfections of God and in contrast is made grossly aware of one's own wretchedness and the wickedness of the world. Moreover, the gifts of holy fear and of piety have already stamped the individual with an ardent desire to please God. The combination of these gifts working together stimulates that hunger for righteousness which is characteristic of the Blessed. For when they were diseased they did not realize their sinful state, and did not hunger and thirst for righteousness. But with the gifts already received they are beginning to enter the way of illumination, which naturally follows upon the way of purgation which is now passing.

The soul has found Jesus and discovers her beloved to be altogether desirable.

> My dove, hiding in the clefts of the rock,
> in the coverts of the cliff,
> show me your face,
> let me hear your voice;
> for your voice is sweet and your face is lovely.
> Catch the foxes for us, the little foxes

that make havoc of the vineyards,
for our vineyards are in fruit. (Song 2:14–15)

It is this apprehension of his beauty that is the source of the desire for righteousness. The soul is beginning to bring forth the fruits of the Spirit, but the "little foxes" of the desire of the flesh, the desire of the eyes, and the pride of life still wreak havoc among her vineyards, the virtues planted by the Spirit, which she has been cultivating. She needs the grace of the Son of God to still her spirit to prepare the soul for the final stage of union.

The more we possess Jesus, the more we desire him. That is true. But the office of the Holy Spirit is such as to bring us into a closer unity with the Son—to be formed into his likeness—that we may then be presented to the Father as a perfect offering. The gifts of the Holy Spirit form us in Christ, for his Holy Spirit is precisely the love of God in act. Spurred on by this love the soul seeks impatiently for righteousness with a bold and urgent spirit because the soul knows it can do nothing of itself, but also knows that all things are possible to those who are in Christ Jesus (Mk. 9:23). Therefore, to further the soul in this desire and this determination, the Holy Spirit helps with the gift of fortitude.

The gift of fortitude is a supernatural *habitus* or faculty which imparts to the will an impulse and an energy which strengthen the soul for the practise of virtue. The soul is invigorated and enthused so that any trace of lukewarmness is erased. Nothing is too difficult and nothing is tedious in the service of God. The soul is enabled to act with unconquerable confidence to overcome any obstacle or peril which may stand in one's path to holiness. It is precisely this confidence which distinguishes this gift from the natural virtue of fortitude: "I can do all things through Christ who strengthens me" (Phil. 4:13). While the cardinal virtue of fortitude gives the soul a capacity for perseverance, the spiritual gift of fortitude imparts the confidence of success. The soul becomes intrepid and valiant as was most clearly exemplified in Ss. Ignatius, John Chrysostom, Hugh of Lincoln, Joan of Arc, Thomas More, Francis Xavier, and Kateri Tekakwitha. Martyrdom is considered the supreme act of this gift, for the person can show no greater love than to offer one's life to

God. Yet, daily to spend and to exert oneself completely for others is in itself a martyrdom hardly less meritorious, which is in the reach of all and is nowise less virtuous. The diligent disciple suffers all these things heroically with patience and joy.

The chief means of cultivating the gift of fortitude, in addition to prayer and self-denial, is frequent reception of the Holy Eucharist. Just as the corporal body gains strength from the nourishment and the sustenance provided by physical food, so the spirit gains grace and fortification from spiritual food. It is principally through the reception of the Holy Eucharist that we may obtain from Jesus the fortitude and patience we need to meet the trials and difficulties of each day. "As the living Father sent me and I draw life from the Father, so whoever eats me will also draw life from me" (Jn. 6:57). St. Chrysostom likens Christians returning from the Lord's Table "as lions breathing fire, terrible to the devil."

Another means of predisposing one to this gift is to accept whatever crosses Our Heavenly Lord is pleased to send us, not asking that they be lifted, but only that we may be given the strength to carry them. For nothing can work against this will of God more than to receive these crosses with complaint. If we refuse to carry our crosses we cannot be disciples of Jesus (Lk. 14:27). Indeed, if we frustrate the operation of the Holy Spirit in this gift, then how can we expect to receive further gifts? We might even be committing the sin of disobeying God. We should never complain about our crosses, but instead we should rejoice in them, that we have been graced with this work of God, that it is his will, and that he will never be outdone in generosity. For God will not ignore our sighs and groans, but out of the honour he holds for his Son, accepts our offering too. "Blessed are you if you suffer for being upright.... If you are insulted for bearing Christ's name, blessed are you, for on you rests the Spirit of God, the Spirit of Glory.... You will only have to suffer for a little while: the God of all grace who called you to eternal glory in Christ will restore you; he will confirm, strengthen and support you. His power lasts forever and ever" (1 Pt. 3:14; 4:14; 5:9–10).

All this is part of the mortification and self-denial followed by all the saints who embraced suffering joyfully as a means of testifying their love. There are many opportunities in everyday life as one ful-fils the duties of one's state or vocation to practise the presence of God in this way. One can gain much merit for oneself and for others in this manner: "For this is merit if, in awareness of God, you bear griefs, suffering unjustly" (1 Pt. 2:19). And the more merit one gains, the more graces one receives, and the more saintly one becomes.

How could Our Lord fail to reward such arduous toil? To our confidence in his generosity and power, God will add the grace of charity. We shall come to love him even more as we experience his ever-present help. Our Lord will become more personal to us: more of a friend. We shall draw closer to him in love as we desire to give to him ever more devotion. We shall happily deny ourselves for him and gladly empty ourselves of all that does not please him; for he will pervade these emptied spaces with himself. What greater bless-ing for those who hunger and thirst for righteousness than they should be filled with the Lord himself?

The gift of counsel and the merciful. The soul's will has already been formed and edified by the three gifts of holy fear, piety, and forti-tude; and the intellect has been illumined by the gift of knowledge. The disciple, now detached and poor in spirit, and having been purged by copious tears, has progressed in blessedness and sanctity. The beatitudes of mourning and yearning for righteousness have prepared the disciple for the higher intellectual gifts and for those beatitudes which will bring one to the threshold of union.

Natural justice is ordinarily perfected by the gift of knowledge, but in order to become like Christ one must progress beyond mere distributive justice—surpass the righteousness of the scribes and the Pharisees—to the beatitude of mercy. To be able to forgive our ene-mies, walk the extra mile, and offer one's very self for the good of others one needs supernatural grace. To take upon ourselves the miseries of those whom we love is natural human kindness, even *pietas*; but to show kindness to the stranger, to have pity for the weak, and to be merciful to one's enemies require the higher gifts. Yet these latter exemplify the heart of God. They are expressive of the Holy Spirit of love who, like the constant sun and the gentle rain, cascades upon all creation the divine goodness. God is merciful because he is infinitely good. How can words describe the infinite plenitude of God who wills, knows, and acts from one simple immense reality? It is the nature of God to give being in all its perfection and fullness. More than any other virtue mercy imitates God.

Mercy is the incarnate characteristic of Jesus: "Not by works of righteousness which we have done, but according to his mercy he saved us, by the washing of regeneration, and renewing of the Holy Ghost; which he shed on us through Jesus Christ our Saviour" (Tt. 3:5). Therefore, we have been called by Mercy to give mercy: "Be merciful, even as your Father is merciful" (Lk. 6:36). In order to practise the superior righteousness which our Lord has described in the Sermon on the Mount, we need the grace of mercy. Mercy is essential to the life of beatitude because it reflects the heart of God, it is of the Spirit of God, and is therefore divine. Moreover, if the soul is to approach unto union with the divine it must grow in this beatitude; for mercy is nothing more than empathy shown to sinners like us who suffer, who need our succor. The merciful feel the sorrows of those who suffer just as Our Lord feels the sorrows of we who mourn because of our need for him. Because their source of illumination is divine, the merciful now begin to feel the pain of the whole world.

Moved by a spirit of compassion upon suffering creatures the disciple—already strengthened with the gift of fortitude still requires a more vivid light to perfect the natural virtue of prudence. Ordinarily the virtue of prudence equips us to seek out the best means-to-end policy, informed by past lessons and experience, in order to reach a wise decision. Prudence directs justice, but the strict distribution of justice without mercy is cruelty. Therefore, to accomplish acts of mercy, which are in proper accord with what is needed (instead of what is justly deserved) a higher, purer source of light, which prudence cannot give, must be imparted to the intellect. The light which the gift of counsel imparts enables the soul to intuit promptly and rightly what must be done in view of supernatural ends. By it the soul perceives misfortunes as God does. The Holy Spirit shows us what ought to be done according to the circumstances of the situation and the moment in which we must respond; and adapts this perfectly to the person concerned.

The soul who operates under the gift of counsel is able to preserve an authentic conscience. The Holy Spirit coordinates all the
gifts so that one's conscience is properly informed as well. Thus,
when the disciple performs those virtuous acts which are also perfectly in accordance with means to end, there can be no violation of
any moral precepts. St. Joan of Arc is a perfect example of this gift.
Her ability to plan and execute strategies, coordinate campaigns,
mobilize an army of men, enthuse them, spiritually direct them and
counsel them wisely, impressed even her contemporaries. When the
Comte de Dunois, commander of the troops at Orleans, tried to
countermand her plans, the Saint replied: "You have been to your
council and I have been to mine. In God's name, the counsel of the
Lord God is wiser and surer than yours."

No matter how difficult the situation, the Holy Spirit through the
gift of counsel provides the solution. If the disciple is perfectly docile and faithful to grace, intent on performing all for the glory of
God, but has come to the limits of reason in the matter, the holy gift
of counsel will enlighten one to act in a manner which reason alone
would not suggest, but which is perfectly apposite to the proper outcome. Human reason is fallible and its practical conclusions uncertain so that it must often proceed slowly and with caution. Yet in the
decisive junctures of our lives the divine Advocate, who assesses all
in a single act of intuition, is able to make us also to see at the
opportune time just what we must do. The soul is guided in this
with security, without mishap, and with assured confidence. Even
more, the disciple performs these acts of mercy with understanding,
compassion, and gentleness. As one penetrates more deeply into the
miseries of others, even so one discovers more resourceful and beneficial means of helping others advance in ways personally sanctifying and fruitful in the virtues.

To dispose oneself to this virtue the disciple needs to discern
humbly one's own weakness and ignorance in order that one may
be moved to resort to the Holy Spirit for his aid. This requires
reflection and self-examination to discover what it is that one lacks
or just why one cannot proceed. From these follow the practice of
listening to God's voice which can be perfected by constantly placing oneself in the presence of God. Finally, we must not grieve the

Holy Spirit (Eph. 4:30), but with docility and meekness obey his promptings; for if we sow in the Spirit we will harvest eternal life (Gal. 6:8).

We have said that mercy is the virtue that makes us most like Christ: for mercy is to suffer with and to suffer for. Mercy places on each of our shoulders a cross which cannot be removed in this life. Endless are those in need of our mercy. This fallen world constantly throws them at our feet, so that for those who are moved by the divine pity there is no rest from this new and seemingly infinite suffering. We are plunged into a sea of compassion and personal pain: for we are imitating Christ in his own passion and death. This purgation is the deepest of all; it is the one that will bring us into Spiritual union with Christ. It will render us most pleasing to our Heavenly Father as the image of his crucified Son is formed in us.

Enlightened by the gift of counsel the disciple perceives the supernatural nature of this virtue: the spirit of mercy is the Spirit of God. One loves with the love of God. One now realizes that one has loved with and in the very Spirit which proceeds from both the Father and the Son, so that all the things which mercy has ever accomplished was but a participation in the life of God. Immersed in the Spirit of God we have drawn from his divine substance. And by the divine inbreathing the Spirit returns our love as a sweet oblation to the Father. The Father receives this offering for the Son's sake, and mercifully returns grace into our souls a hundredfold. This communion is mutually penetrating, a real exchange of hearts. The soul serves God with all her faculties and with all her strength; and God blesses the soul by pouring himself out in the Holy Spirit. "Blessed are the merciful for they shall receive mercy."

The gift of understanding and the pure of heart. The temple of God cannot be impure. Holiness cannot long abide its contrary; nor can evil bear the light of purity. Since God is infinite holiness, infinite and absolute perfection, then impurity is simply whatever is not of God. Being excludes non-being. God is one simple, infinite, indefectible reality and, therefore, subsists in consummate light, a light so encompassing as to admit of no limitation: "God is light, and in him is no darkness at all" (1 Jn. 1:5). The infinite holiness of God, which excludes all that is impure, is identical to his infinite brightness. Light and purity are two semblances of the one divine reality: a reality which is perfectly translucent to itself. There is no "part" of God's Being which is not available to his pervasive illumination. Like two mirrors facing each other to produce an infinity of reflections, so God understands himself: "God from God, light from light. . . ." This is the mystery of the divine self-knowing in which what God is and what God knows is encompassed in his own singular effulgence: "who alone has immortality, who dwells in unapproachable light, whom no one has ever seen or can see" (1 Tim. 6:16).

Now, to be pure of heart is to have a heart emptied of all that is not God: to desire God only. For where one's treasure is, there is one's heart. And so those who are of a pure heart, singularly devoted to God, will be filled with his light. Truly to be pure of heart is to see God.

However, such a vision of God is not possible for anyone in this life: "No one has seen the Father except the one who is from God; only he has seen the Father" (Jn. 6:46). Therefore, in order for the pure in heart to see God a supernatural gift is necessary—the gift of understanding. St. Thomas[5] teaches that there are two stages in seeing God. One is imperfect which sees God according to what he is not and which enables us to comprehend how far God is beyond our comprehension. The second is a perfect vision by which God's essence is seen and which is consummated only in Heaven. The first enables us to grasp God incompletely in an analogous way proportional to the perfections we perceive in creatures. The second is the Beatific Vision reserved for the saints and heavenly angels. Both visions correspond to the gift of understanding.

The gift of understanding enables us to know God more perfectly. This gift differs from that of knowledge in two fundamental ways. Firstly, while knowledge concerns created things, understanding extends to all the revealed truths. Secondly, the insight which understanding gives is much deeper. While knowledge enabled us to grasp created things according to their perfections and their ordering before God, this gift enlightens us to grasp the sense of divine truths

---

5. *Summa Theol.* IIa IIae. q. 8, a. 7.

and their mutual consistency and significance. Thus the gift of understanding is a supernatural habit, infused in the soul under the enlightening action of the Holy Spirit, which gives us a profound insight into revealed truths according to their supernatural end.

It does this in six ways according to St. Thomas:[6] 1) It discloses to us the substance hidden beneath the accidents, for example, the body of Christ beneath the Eucharistic species. 2) It illuminates the meaning of the holy scriptures as our Lord did for the disciples on the way to Emmaus. 3) It makes apparent the signification of the language of sensible signs, giving us an insight into the analogous nature of these things: e.g., the analogy of baptism with dying to sin, or Christ's resurrection with that of new life in the Spirit. 4) Similarly, it communicates the capacity to see spiritual realities beneath the outward appearance: we have a deeper penetration into the divinity of Jesus, for example. 5) We are able to see the effects contained in their causes as in the more pervasive benefits and blessings of the Sacraments, the Church, prayer, and sacrifice. 6) Finally, we are able to comprehend the divine providence behind even the ordinary happenings of our lives as well as in the larger events in the world.

By far the greatest endowment of the gift of understanding is that penetrating insight into the truths of faith: sufficient for us only to the extent that we become confirmed in our belief, but not to full comprehension of the divine mysteries. Even though we are still wayfarers in the state of faith, nevertheless nothing in the outward appearance of things hinders us from believing those things which fall under faith (*de fide*) such as the Trinity, the incarnation, the four last things, etc. Furthermore, a greater number of doctrines and precepts are brought under the light of our understanding so that we are better able to explain them to others and to demonstrate their necessity and effectiveness. "Give me understanding and I shall learn your commandments" (Ps. 119: 73).

In order to dispose ourselves for this gift we must prepare ourselves for the illumination of the Holy Spirit who will lead us into all truth. This requires that we practise a lively and simple faith in

6. *Summa Theol.* IIa IIae. q. 8, a. 1.

all that the Church, tradition, and holy scripture reveal to us. Because light cannot exist alongside darkness nor purity with impurity, so we must also keep ourselves pure in soul and in body. We must maintain ourselves in a state of grace, purging ourselves of all ideas and actions contrary to the teachings of the Church, which is the spouse of the Holy Spirit. We must remove all dissipation and worldliness, emptying ourselves of attachment to creatures and withdrawing into the secret cloisters of our souls to dwell there in the presence of the Holy Spirit of God. And we must invoke the Holy Spirit with a heart willingly submissive to his grace. It is the pure in heart who will see God: in this life, in the obscurity of faith illuminated by the supernatural light of the gift of understanding; and in the next life in the beatific vision of God.

Our Blessed Lord has confirmed for us this truth: "I bless you, Father, Lord of heaven and earth, for hiding these things from the learned and the clever and revealing them to little children" (Mt. 11:25). It is through a childlike trust and the simplicity of faith that we will enter the kingdom of heaven (Mt. 18:3). For who is more pure than these little ones? The arrogance, so apparent in our contemporary evil culture, presumes upon the truth; although it is so evident how frequently that truth has been overlooked or misunderstood. This blindness would arouse our pity were it not so deliberate and deadly. But the secret to surpassing the professed righteousness of our present-day scribes and Pharisees—those among us who distort or undermine sacred truth—is to be receptive to the divine gift of understanding and to have compassion on those who do not or will not understand. Here is irony: that "God has chosen the foolish things of the world to confound the wise; and God has chosen the weak things of the world to shame the mighty" (1 Cor. 1:27). But what could be more apparent than, that by receiving the Holy Spirit and his gifts, we are led into truth as well? For it is his office to bring us to Christ the Son, the incarnate Word. There can be no contradiction between the teachings of the Holy Spirit and those of Christ. Indeed, there can be no discord between the doctrines of the Church and the saints. No wonder it is the pure in heart who will see God, for it is they who will have made room for his Spirit.

The gift of wisdom and the blessing of peace. Our minds and hearts were not formed for created things. Our nobility of intellect is not confined to them, because it can transcend the finite and rise to the one, the true, the good, and the beautiful. Nor can the world, being finite and imperfect, ever satisfy or pacify our souls for we, having been made in the image of God, are destined for heavenly things. Also, we have been baptized in the Holy Spirit and, therefore, are the temples of the Blessed Trinity. Now, serenity and harmony are characteristic of the three Persons of the Trinity who are one in Spirit. So, having received the gifts of the Holy Spirit, all our members and faculties are properly ordered with the consequence that our souls are blessed with peace. For it is one of the fruits of the Holy Spirit: "the fruit of the Holy Spirit is love, joy, peace...." (Gal. 5:22). Peace, says St. Augustine in his *City of God*, is the tranquillity of order. Where there is no opposition, no conflict or discord, peace reigns. When all things are duly ordered to each other and to God, then peace pervades our souls.

With order brought to the motions of our hearts and everything subordinated to mind and to spirit, with our house stilled and peace reigning within our hearts; we are then able to communicate our peace to others. Having been graced with the cardinal virtues of prudence, justice, temperance, and fortitude; and the theological virtues of faith, hope, and charity; as well as the seven gifts of the Holy Spirit, the disciple is truly of the kingdom of blessedness and is best fitted to be a peacemaker. For those who love peace are the sons of peace, since they are children of their heavenly Father. "The blessedness of the peacemakers is the reward of adoption, 'they shall be called the sons of God.' For God is our common parent, and no other way can we pass into his family than by living in brotherly love together."[7]

"Peace I leave with you; my peace I give to you. Not as the world gives do I give to you. Let not your hearts be troubled, neither let them be afraid" (Jn. 14:27). Peace like this is a divine gift which only wisdom and love can bring forth. The final gift of the Holy Spirit is the gift of wisdom which perfects the theological virtue of charity.

---

7. St. Hilary, quoted in *Catena Aurea*, Mt. ch. 5.

Thus, wisdom resides in both the intellect and the will. It is a supernatural light which enables us rightly to discern God and divine matters in their ultimate principles and highest causes. Wisdom, like the rays of the sun, illuminates the intellect giving it insight into divine truths; and it warms the heart, inflaming it with love and filling it with joy and delight.

> For Wisdom is quicker to move than any motion;
> she is so pure, she pervades and permeates all things.
> She is a breath of the power of God,
> pure emanation of the glory of the Almighty;
> so nothing impure can find its way into her.
> For she is a reflection of the eternal light,
> untarnished mirror of God's active power,
> and image of his goodness. (Wis. 7:24–26)

Therefore, says St. Thomas, "the gift of wisdom corresponds more to charity which unites man's mind to God."[8] Because it belongs to the gift of wisdom to contemplate the divine and since this entails a degree of union with the divine, it follows that wisdom is inseparable from charity. It is the essence of love to seek union with the Beloved; and it is for this reason that the Holy Spirit is the Person to whom this gift is appropriated since love is a fruit of the Holy Spirit who is also the Spirit of truth: "when the Spirit of truth comes he will lead you to the complete truth, since he will not be speaking of his own accord, but will say only what he has been told; and he will reveal to you, the things to come. He will glorify me…" (Jn. 16:13–14).

What is true wisdom if not the glory of Christ revealed to us by the Holy Spirit? There is no higher gift than to taste the beauty and blessedness of the Lord (Ps. 34:8). And on this earth there is no greater life than to be united in the grace of Jesus Christ, the love of God, and the fellowship of the Holy Spirit, whose office is to reproduce Christ in our souls. We, in beholding his glory, are thus to be transformed into his very image by his Spirit (2 Cor. 3:18). This transformation into the living image of Jesus is a participation in

---

8. *Summa Theol.* IIa IIae. q. 9, a. 2, ad 1.

the eternal Wisdom of the Father. At this stage everything converges in this pre-eminent gift of wisdom: for in its light we behold the glory of the Son and are drawn by the love of the Holy Spirit into a deeper union with our heavenly Father.

Clearly such a gift exceeds any knowledge attainable by human learning or natural ability. Thus it is evident that this gift, being available to everyone through the liberality and benevolence of the Holy Spirit, can impart even to a simple and uneducated person a profounder and more comprehensive understanding than the most eminent theologian. Blessed Brother Giles, third companion of St. Francis of Assisi, once asked St. Bonaventure: "Can an ignorant person love God as perfectly as a great scholar?" St. Bonaventure answered: "A poor illiterate old woman may love him more than the most learned doctor in theology." At this Bl. Giles, overcome with zest and exultation of spirit, rushed to the garden gate leading out into the city of Rome, and cried out to the populace: "Listen, poorest, most simple, and most illiterate old woman! Love the Lord our God, and you may become holier and higher and happier than Brother Bonaventure." Then Bl. Giles himself was rapt in ecstasy, and remained motionless for three hours.

Of course, it does not follow that one may claim a special revelation of the Spirit which contradicts the teaching of the Church or that of holy scripture; for these being divinely inspired cannot be at variance with any private understanding (2 Cor. 11:4; Gal. 1:8). The Holy Spirit does not contradict himself. But if one should receive some insight into a divine truth which is in perfect harmony with scripture, tradition, and magisterial teaching, then one can in confidence accept its authenticity. For the mystical state is not something extraordinary in the normal life of the Christian. On the contrary, "it is the normal atmosphere that grace demands, so that it can develop in all its virtualities."[9]

Wisdom, therefore, differs from both the gift of knowledge and understanding. It differs from knowledge in that the latter is related to creatures whereas wisdom is ordered to the things of God. It differs from understanding because the latter concerns divine things

---

9. Jordan Aumann, *Spiritual Theology* (London: Sheed and Ward, 1980), p. 271.

only in their mutual relationships, but not according to their ultimate causes. Furthermore, understanding involves the mind only, while wisdom is an experience of the heart. Wisdom is the most perfect gift because it is more expansive than the intellect, is able to sound greater depths, and can intuit what discursive reason cannot.

In addition to the expansion of charity in the heart and the mystical lights to the intellect, the gift of wisdom perfects the other theological virtues. Perfected by the gift of wisdom, charity diffuses divine grace over these virtues, because charity is the formative principle of all the virtues. This divine influence extends to the entire supernatural organism, so that the whole person is transformed in Christ.

It gives the devoted soul an unshakable faith. Because of its connaturality with divine things, wisdom lends a quasi-experimental knowledge of the truths of revelation, since it is a knowledge that does not rise above the order of faith. It is not an immediate vision of God, since this knowledge is the result of faith illumined by the gifts of the Holy Spirit. Instead, it is faith penetrating and tasting the mysteries of God in accordance with the text: "Taste and see that the Lord is sweet" (Ps. 34:8). Thus faith becomes certain because wisdom has illumined her mysteries and the soul can see their implications and interconnections.

Faith having thus been reinforced, the virtue of hope is more firmly established. With the experience of having been incorporated into the body of Christ we cannot fail but to trust in his promise that he will go ahead of us to establish a place for us. We are members of his kingdom through and in the Holy Spirit. Since we know that he is Our Lord in Heaven with the saints who are already with him, we cannot fail to hope in his promises.

By reason of its excellence and sublimity, its elevation and grandeur, wisdom bestows upon the divinized soul many other benefits as well:[10] Wisdom gives to these saints a divine sense of judgement. They perceive everything from God's perspective, penetrating to the supreme cause of all things. The gift of wisdom centres the divinized soul, informed by charity, in the intimacy of the divine Persons, in

10. Ibid., pp. 272–273.

whom it rests and from whom it acts. The soul now lives in union with the Blessed Trinity being caught up in the triune life. As a result the soul can begin to practise virtue to a heroic degree. Freed from human limitations these saints can perform those acts which are not only extreme, such as prolonged fasting, vigils, prayer, and prolonged meritorious works; but also miraculous actions such as healing, bi-location, or the reading of hearts and minds. Wisdom also enables us to practise the moral virtues to the highest degree. No longer do worldly things hold any relish for us. We love the cross, mortification, effort, service, purity, the sacraments, the mass, etc. because by these means we become more closely identified with Our Blessed Lord and in them are able to demonstrate our love for him.

This supreme and august gift of supernatural wisdom is impossible to obtain through our own efforts: it is truly a divine gift. But as with the other gifts there are means by which we may prepare ourselves for its inception. First, we must become devoted to the Holy Spirit. Devotion to the Holy Spirit is the chief means by which the soul may pass through the narrow door to Our Lord's infinite treasury. From this treasury, the Holy Spirit dispenses copious graces with boundless liberality and delight. It is the nature of infinite Love to give, for goodness is diffusive of itself. Thus souls who are especially devoted to the Holy Spirit are assured of receiving special graces. Pope Leo XIII, in his encyclical of May 9, 1897, writes: "We earnestly desire that . . . piety may increase and be inflamed toward the Holy Spirit, to whom especially all of us owe the grace of following the path of truth and virtue."

Secondly, we must then ardently pray for the gift of wisdom as did King Solomon:

> God of our ancestors, Lord of mercy, who by your word have made the universe, and in your wisdom have fitted human beings to rule the creatures that you have made, to govern the world in holiness and saving justice and in honesty of soul to dispense fair judgement, grant me Wisdom, consort of your throne, and do not reject me from the number of your children. (Wis. 9:1–4)

To ask for this gift gives honour to the Holy Spirit and acknowledges our humility and need. This disposition is very meritorious for its openness and expression of faith.

Thirdly, we must desire this gift for the sake of Jesus Christ and for his Church. To seek wisdom is not a selfish desire, since its purpose is the extension of charity and the dispensing of grace. Wisdom proceeds from the Father as the divine Son, who then became incarnate in Christ Jesus. Immediately, incarnate Wisdom immolated himself for our sakes and ascended to the Father so that the Holy Spirit may be poured out upon us. Since this is the loving intention of the Triune God then it is certain that Wisdom "anticipates those who desire her by making herself known first" (Wis. 6:13). Desire wisdom, then, with all your heart and you will be assured of its bestowal.

These are the extraordinary graces which wisdom perfects in our souls. This is the life in which we are invited to participate. Wisdom emanates from the Father as the Son, who in turn forms the Love of the Holy Spirit which then transforms our hearts. Made perfect in love, we may then, in the charity of the Holy Spirit, return our hearts to God. This exchange of hearts, in which we are, as it were, breathing the life of the Blessed Trinity, is known as transforming union. Many saints, such as St. John of the Cross, have described this remarkable exchange: "When God grants this supernatural favour to the soul, so great a union is caused that all the things of both God and the soul become one in participant transformation, and the soul appears to be God more than a soul."[11] Of course, the soul is not God in substance, but by participation. As St. Teresa of Avila attests, the soul has been drawn into the heart of the life of the Blessed Trinity where in the vivid illumination of her intellect the soul apprehends the Trinity:

> It sees these three Persons, individually, and yet, by a wonderful kind of knowledge which is given to it, the soul realises that most certainly and truly all these three Persons are one Substance and one Power and one Knowledge and one God alone; so that what we hold by faith the soul may be said here to grasp by sight, although nothing is seen by the eyes, either of the body or of the soul, for it is no imaginary vision. Here all three Persons communicate themselves to the soul and speak to the soul and explain to

11. *The Ascent of Mount Carmel,* Bk. 2, cp. 5.

it those words which the Gospel attributes to the Lord, namely, that he and the Father and the Holy Spirit will come to dwell with the soul which loves him and keeps his commandments.[12]

The soul who has reached this state will have achieved perfect peace; for concomitant with the prayer of union is the soul's confirmation in grace. This must be understood as the grace and assistance given by the Holy Spirit to resist all mortal sin as well as a moral certitude of salvation. Whoever has this grace is an adopted son because, having been transformed into living images of the eternal Wisdom, they have become identified with all the motions of his Blessed Spirit. They belong to God: they are called children of God.

⊕

"Fear not, little flock, for it is your Father's good pleasure
to give you the kingdom" (Lk. 12:32).

We have ascended the mountain of the Lord to its level place where we have sat at the Blessed feet of the Holy One of God and we are overawed at his teaching; but also, perhaps, somewhat overwhelmed at its ponderous demands. We are not worthy of so great a blessing. Yet the beatitudes are ours: they are the essential assets of those who belong to the kingdom. The gate, the narrow door, to the kingdom is our Blessed Lord and Saviour. To those who place their whole trust in him he has promised to give the kingdom with all its blessings. He shall do this. Bit by bit, ever so slowly we shall spiral upwards. As long as we persevere in the ascent, blessedness is ours.

The kingdom is our reward and it comes with its various facets. Initially, with that holy fear, which is just the beginning of wisdom, the kingdom of Heaven belongs to those poor in spirit who know their need of God. Next comes the gift of piety given to the meek who will have the earth for their inheritance; for with their *pietas* they belong to the family of God. Knowledge brings comfort to those who have mourned for their sins and the dissipation of their lives. They know they have dishonored the things of their Father's

---

12. *The Interior Castle, Seventh Mansions*, cp. I.

house. But they see all creatures under God and themselves likewise dependent upon him for all that he shall most lovingly give. And they are comforted for they know they are secure in his unfailing care. Those who hunger and thirst for righteousness are already illuminated with insight and the beginnings of supernatural charity: for they realize the beauty and goodness of the Lord and they desire these for all humanity. Yet fortitude is given them that they may labour for their salvation and that of others. And then to the merciful, whose hearts most resemble the heart of the Lord who would die yet again for them if he could, comes the gift of counsel, given to them that they may perfect their acts of mercy. Already those made pure in heart shall have been blessed with the capacity of glimpsing God by means of the gift of understanding. Enabled to penetrate the truths of the faith, mounting truth upon truth and aided by the gift of wisdom, who is the eternal Son of the Father, they will climb to the rarefied atmosphere of his peace. Transformed in the likeness of God, they are his children.

The people of God, the *anawim*, the poor in the Lord, are in their meekness and lowliness most like him who took on the weakness of human nature, and as a tiny child entered our human condition with all its sufferings and oppression. And like him they shall be persecuted, for no longer do they belong to the world. Because the character of Christ is reflected in his disciples, these faithful servants are its accusers, convicting the world of guilt. For this reason the world hates the children of God. However, by turning our sufferings into a prayer we are united in the summit of our souls, through faith, with the passion of Christ. Our sufferings mark our identity with Jesus. This wicked world is not our home. Rather, our home is the kingdom of Heaven. "Blessed are you when men shall revile you, and persecute you, and shall say all manner of evil against you falsely, for my sake. Rejoice, and be exceedingly glad: for great is your reward in Heaven."

The *principium* which establishes the kingdom of Heaven is the supremacy of Jesus himself: a pre-eminence and majesty which he holds and will bestow on those truly united with him through the Holy Spirit. Along with this grace comes a vital intimacy since faith has connected us to that point in our souls where Our Lord dwells establishing his kingdom within us. This communion becomes the wellspring of all virtue and holiness which inform all those who through faith are made citizens of his kingdom: the people of his covenant. And insofar as we are receptive to all which he pleases to grant us, so we are conformed to him in the highest point of our souls. Our Lord Jesus, who is all beatitude and light, providentially guards a tiny spark in the apex of the soul, which is sufficient and efficacious in bringing all who continue to place their trust in him to an assured salvation: for those who persevere to the end will be saved. Yet unlike Moses before the burning bush or the children of Israel beneath the fiery summit of Horeb, we who have stood, as it were, on the Mount of Beatitudes are more than privileged, because "we have beheld His glory, the glory of the only begotten Son of the Father, full of grace and truth." Our treasure in Heaven!

Appendix 1

The Replies of the Pontifical Biblical Commission on Questions of Sacred Scripture

From Denzinger, *Enchiridion Symbolorum.*
Thirteenth edition, tr. by Roy J. Deferrari. Fitzwilliam:
Loreto Publications, 1955.

The Author, the Date, and the Historical Truth of the Gospel according to Matthew

[Response of the Biblical Commission, June 19, 1911]

2148 I. Whether after noting the universal and constant agreement of the Church from the earliest times, which is clearly shown by the eloquent testimonies of the Fathers, the inscriptions of the manuscripts of the Gospels, even the most ancient versions of the Sacred Scriptures, and the catalogues handed down by the Holy Fathers, the ecclesiastical writers, the Highest Pontiffs, and the Councils, and finally the liturgical practice of the Eastern and Western Church, it can and should be affirmed with certainty that Matthew, the Apostle of Christ, is in fact the author of the vulgate Gospel under his name?—Reply: In the affirmative.

2149 II. Whether the opinion should be considered as sufficiently supported by the assent of tradition, which holds that Matthew preceded the other evangelists in his writing, and that he composed the first Gospel in the native language then employed by the Jews of Palestine, to whom that work was directed?—Reply: In the affirmative to both parts.

2150 III. Whether the redaction of this original text can be placed beyond the time of the overthrow of Jerusalem, so that the prophecies which are read there about this same overthrow were written after the event; or whether what is customarily alleged to be the testimony of Irenaeus [Adv. haer., lib.3, cap.I, n.2] of uncertain and controversial interpretation, is to be considered of such weight that it forces us to reject the opinion of those who think, more in accord with tradition, that the same redaction was composed even before Paul's arrival in the City? —Reply: In the negative to both parts.

2151 IV. Whether that opinion of certain moderns can even with some probability be sustained, according to which Matthew did not properly or strictly compose the Gospel such as has been handed down to us, but only some collection of the words or conversations of Christ, which another anonymous author has made use of as sources, whom they make the redactor of the Gospel itself.—Reply: In the negative.

2152 V. Whether from the fact that the Fathers and all ecclesiastical writers, indeed the Church herself from her own incunabula used, as canonical, only the Greek text of the Gospel known under the name of Matthew, not even excepting those who taught expressly that Matthew the Apostle wrote in his native language, it can be proved with certainty that the Greek Gospel is identical as to substance with that Gospel written in his native language by the same Apostle?—Reply: In the affirmative.

The Authors, Dates, and Historical Truth of the Gospels according to Mark and Luke

[Reply of the Biblical Commission, June 26, 1912]

2155 I. Whether the evident judgment of tradition, from the beginnings of the Church in wonderful agreement with and confirmed by manifold arguments, namely, the eloquent testimonies of the Holy Fathers and ecclesiastical writers, the citations and allusions which occur in the writings of the same, the practice of the ancient heretics, the versions of the Books of the New Testament, the most ancient and almost entire body of manuscripts, and also the internal reasons taken from the very text of the Sacred Books, definitely compels the affirmation that Mark, the disciple and expounder of Peter, and

Luke the physician, the hearer and companion of Paul, are in fact the authors of the Gospels which are respectively attributed to them?— Reply: In the affirmative.

2159 V. Whether, with respect to the chronological order of the Gospels, it is right to withdraw from that opinion which, strengthened equally by the most ancient and continued testimony of tradition, testifies that Mark was the second in order to write and Luke the third, after Matthew, who was the first of all to write his Gospel in his native tongue; or, whether their opinion, which asserts that the Gospel was composed second and third before the Greek version of the first Gospel, is to be regarded in turn as in opposition to this idea?—Reply: In the negative to both parts.

2160 VI. Whether the time of composition of the Gospel of Mark and Luke may be postponed until the overthrow of the city of Jerusalem; or, because the prophecy of the Lord in Luke about the overthrow of this city seems more definite, it can be sustained that his Gospel at least was composed after the siege had already begun?— Reply: In the negative to both parts.

2161 VII. Whether it ought to be affirmed that the Gospel of Luke preceded the book of the *Acts of the Apostles*; and although this book, with same author Luke [Acts 1:1 ff.], was finished before the end of the Apostle's Roman captivity [Acts 28:30ff.], his Gospel was not composed after this time?—Reply: In the affirmative.

On the Synoptic Problem or the Mutual Relations of the First Three Gospels

[Reply of the Biblical Commission, June 26, 1912]

2164 I. Whether, preserving what must be jealously preserved according to the decisions made above, especially on the authenticity and integrity of the three Gospels of Matthew, Mark, and Luke; on the substantial identity of the Greek Gospel of Matthew with its early original; also on the order of time in which the same were written, to explain their mutual likenesses and differences, midst so many varying and opposite opinions of the authors, it is permitted for exegetes to dispute freely and to appeal to the hypotheses of tradition whether written or oral, or even of the dependence of one upon a preceding or upon several preceding?—Reply: In the affirmative.

2165 II. Whether they should be advised to preserve what was established above, who, supported by no testimony of tradition or by historical argument, easily taken in by the hypothesis publicly proclaimed of two sources, which labors to explain the composition of the Greek Gospel of Matthew and of the Gospel of Luke chiefly by their dependence upon the Gospel of Mark and a so-called collection of the Lord's discourses; and whether they are thus able to defend this freely?—Reply. In the negative to both parts.

The Author, the Date, and the Historical Truth of the Acts of the Apostles

[Reply of the Biblical Commission, June 12, 1913]

2166 I. Whether in view especially of the tradition of the whole Church going back to the earliest ecclesiastical writers, and noting the internal reasons of the book of Acts, considered in itself or in its relation to the third Gospel, and especially because of the mutual affinity and connection between the two prologues [Luke 1:1–4; Acts 1:1ff.], it must be held as certain that the volume that is entitled Actus Apostolorum, or, (Greek text deleted), has Luke the Evangelist as author?—Reply: In the affirmative.

2167 II. Whether for critical reasons taken from the language and style, and from the manner of narrating, and from the oneness of aim and doctrine, it can be demonstrated that the book of the Acts of the Apostles should be attributed to one author alone; and therefore that the opinion of more recent writers which holds that Luke is not the only author of the book, but that different persons are to be recognized as authors of the same book is devoid of any foundation?—Reply: In the affirmative to both parts.

2168 III. Whether in outward appearance, the prominent chapters in the Acts where the use of the third person is broken off and the first person plural introduced, weaken the unity and authenticity of composition; or rather historically and philologically considered are to be said to confirm it?—Reply: In the negative to the first part; in the affirmative to the second.

2169 IV. Whether because of the fact that the book itself is abruptly concluded after scarcely making mention of the two years of Paul's first Roman captivity, it may be inferred that the author had written a second volume now lost, or had intended to write it; and so the time of composition of the Book of Acts can be deferred long after this captivity; or whether it should rather rightly and worthily be held that Luke toward the end of the first Roman captivity of the Apostle Paul had completed his book?—Reply: In the negative to the first part; in the affirmative to the second.

Appendix 2

A Note on the Sermon in *The Didache*

The Didache (teaching, instruction) was discovered in 1873 by Philotheos Brynnios, Metropolitan of Nicomedia. Eusebius mentions it as the *Teaching of the Apostles* (*HE* 3.25.1) as does Athanasius in his *Festal Letter* (39). Coptic and Ethiopian translations were also later discovered. The work reflects a very primitive Christian community. For example, the Eucharistic prayers are very closely modelled on Jewish forms of grace with no mention of the Last Supper or, for that matter, of the traditional Eucharistic formula given in 1 Cor. 11:23–27. The description of the ministry is also primitive. Chapters 11–12 portray an itinerant ministry of "apostles" (with no mention of the "Twelve") as well as prophets and teachers, while ch. 15 urges the community to choose bishops and deacons "for they are carrying out the ministry of the prophets and teachers for you. Do not esteem them lightly. . . ." Nevertheless, it is the prophets who minister to them and who are still to be considered their "High

Priests" (13). This unsettled structure of the priesthood clearly does not accord with the status afforded to that more institutionalized bishopric already functional in the second century. Also there is an exhortation to prepare oneself for the coming of the Lord, which is reminiscent of the description of Christian beliefs given by Paul in 2 Thess. 2:1–12. Finally, in ch. 8 there is an admonition to distance oneself from what appear to be Degaussers (*ioudaïzein* in Gal. 2:14)—i.e., those who were members of the Pharisaic party who become believers—which is reminiscent of the community just as it is presented in Acts 15. Thus, the picture of the early Church given in *The Didache* fits in well with what we know of the communities towards the mid to latter part of the first century.

The Didache is divided into two parts: "The Two Ways" and "A Manual for the Church." But it is in the first part that we find most of the several verses that repeat the teachings of Our Lord in the Sermon on the Mount. Here mention is made of several of Our Lord's precepts such as: turning the other cheek, giving up one's shirt when asked for one's coat, walking the extra mile, warning against adultery and giving false witness, an exhortation to "be meek for the meek are to inherit the earth" (3), and not to parade one's merits or judge unjustly, as well as the "golden rule"—at least twenty closely-worded verses from Matthew's Gospel. Also in part two there is a form of the Lord's Prayer which closely follows that presented in Matthew rather than the form given in Luke.

Despite the sundry similarities between *The Didache* and Matthew, it is not evident that either one depends upon the other, or that they both possibly represent a similar, more primitive *oral* tradition received from within the same geographical and cultural setting. Both do portray a Jewish Christian ethos struggling with Pharisaic issues, however. Also, the agreements between the Trinitarian baptismal formula in *The Didache* (7) and Matthew (Mt. 28:19) as well as the similar construction of the Lord's Prayer (Did. 8 and Mt. 6:5–13) appear to express homogeneous traditions. Finally, both *The Didache* (11–13) and Matthew's Sermon (7:15–20) warn to beware of deceptive itinerant apostles and prophets.

Bibliography

Aquinas, St. Thomas, *Catena Aurea: Commentary on the Four Gospels.* Vol. I. St. Matthew. Tr. John Henry Newman. Oxford: Veritatis Splendor Publications, 2012.

Augustine, St. *On Christian Doctrine.* Chicago: The Great Books. 1952.

_____. *On the Sermon on the Mount.* Marston Gate: Limovia.net, 2013.

Aumann, Jordan. *Spiritual Theology.* London: Sheed and Ward, 1980.

Benedict XVI. *Jesus of Nazereth: From the Baptism in the Jordan to the Transfiguration.* London: Bloomsbury, 2007.

Cantalamessa, Raniero. *Beatitudes: Eight Steps to Happiness.* Cincinnati: Servant Books, 2009.

Carson, D.A. *Exegetical Fallacies.* Grand Rapids: Baker Book House, 1987.

Collins, Thomas Archbishop. *Pathway to our Hearts: A Simple Approach to Lectio Devina with the Sermon on the Mount.* Notre Dame: Ave Maria Press, 2011.

Congar, Yves. *The Meaning of Tradition.* San Francisco: Ignatius Press, 2004.

Daniélou, Jean. *God and the Ways of Knowing.* San Francisco: Ignatius Press, 2003.

De Lubac, Henri. *Medieval Exegesis: The Four Senses of Scripture.* Vol. 1. Tr. By Mark Sebanc. Grand Rapids: Wm. B. Eerdmans, 1998.

_____. *Medieval Exegesis: The Four Senses of Scripture.* Vol. 2. Tr. By E.M. Macierwoski. Grand Rapids: Wm. B. Eerdmans, 2000.

Ford, Clayton Howard. *Who Really Wrote the Bible?* Mustang, Oklahoma: Tate Publishing, 2009.

Granados, José *et al. Opening Up the Scriptures: Joseph Ratzinger and the Foundations of Biblical Interpretation.* Grand Rapids: Wm. B. Eerdmans, 2008.

Guardini, Romano Cardinal. *The Lord.* Washington: Regnery Publishing Inc., 1998.

Hamm, Dennis S.J. *Building Our House on Rock: The Sermon on the Mount as Jesus' Vision for Our Lives.* Frederick, Maryland: 2011.

Harrington, Daniel J. *The Gospel of Matthew (Sacra Pagina).* Collegeville: The Liturgical Press, 1991.

Hendriksen, William. *The Gospel of Matthew.* Edinburgh: Banner of Truth, 1976.

John Paul II, St. *Blessed are the Pure in Heart: Catechesis on the Sermon on the Mount.* Boston: Daughters of St. Paul, 1983.

Krentz, Edgar. *The Historical-Critical Method.* Philadelphia: Fortress Press, 1975.

Maier, Gerhard. *The End of the Historical-Critical Method.* St. Louis: Concordia, 1977.

Martinez, Archbishop Luis M. *The Sanctifier.* Boston: Daughters of St. Paul, 2003.

Mitch, Curtis and Sri, Edward. *The Gospel of Matthew.* Grand Rapids: Baker, 2010.

Morris, Leon. *Luke.* London: Inter-Varsity Press, 1974.

Quarles, Charles. *The Sermon on the Mount: Restoring Christ's Message to the Modern Church.* Nashville: B & H Academic, 2011.

Schnackenburg, Rudolf. *The Gospel of Matthew.* Cambridge: Wm. B. Eerdmans, 2002.

Sheen, Fulton J. *The Cross and the Beatitudes.* Missouri, Ligouri, 2000.

Stein, Robert H. *The Synoptic Problem.* Grand Rapids, Baker, 1987.

Tanquerry, Adolphe. *The Spiritual Life: A Treatise on Ascetical and Mystical Theology.* Baltimore: St. Mary's Seminary, 1930.

Vann, Gerald. *The Divine Pity: A Study in the Social Implications of the Beatitudes.* London: Fontana, 1945.

_____. *The Pain of Christ and the Sorrow of God.* NY: Alba House, 1999.

Wansbrough, Henry OSB. *The Use and Abuse of the Bible: A Brief History of Biblical Interpretation.* London: T&T Clark, 2011.

Wenham, John. *Redating Matthew, Mark & Luke: A Fresh Assault on the Synoptic Problem.* London: Hodder & Stoughton, 1991.

Wesley, John. *Sermons.* Vols. I & II. Grand Rapids: Francis Asbury Press, 1955.

www.ingramcontent.com/pod-product-compliance
Lightning Source LLC
Chambersburg PA
CBHW021504090426
42739CB00007B/457